Get started
in Korean

Jaehoon Yeon

First published in Great Britain in 2013 by Hodder & Stoughton. An Hachette UK company.

First published in US in 2013 by The McGraw-Hill Companies, Inc.

Copyright © Jaehoon Yeon 2013

The right of Jaehoon Yeon to be identified as the Author of the Work has been asserted by her in accordance with the Copyright, Designs and Patents Act 1988.

Database right Hodder Education (makers)

The *Teach Yourself* name is a registered trademark of Hachette UK.

All rights reserved. No part of this publication may be reproduced, stored in a retrieval system or transmitted in any form or by any means, electronic, mechanical, photocopying, recording or otherwise, without the prior written permission of the publisher, or as expressly permitted by law, or under terms agreed with the appropriate reprographic rights organization. Enquiries concerning reproduction outside the scope of the above should be sent to the Rights Department, Hodder & Stoughton, at the address below.

You must not circulate this book in any other binding or cover and you must impose this same condition on any acquirer.

British Library Cataloguing in Publication Data: a catalogue record for this title is available from the British Library.

Library of Congress Catalog Card Number: on file.

10 9 8 7 6 5 4 3 2 1

The publisher has used its best endeavours to ensure that any website addresses referred to in this book are correct and active at the time of going to press. However, the publisher and the author have no responsibility for the websites and can make no guarantee that a site will remain live or that the content will remain relevant, decent or appropriate.

The publisher has made every effort to mark as such all words which it believes to be trademarks. The publisher should also like to make it clear that the presence of a word in the book, whether marked or unmarked, in no way affects its legal status as a trademark.

Every reasonable effort has been made by the publisher to trace the copyright holders of material in this book. Any errors or omissions should be notified in writing to the publisher, who will endeavour to rectify the situation for any reprints and future editions.

Cover image © Madeleine Openshaw / Shutterstock

Typeset by Cenveo® Publisher Services.

Printed in China for Hodder & Stoughton, an Hachette Livre UK company, 338 Euston Road, London, NW1 3BH.

Hodder & Stoughton policy is to use papers that are natural, renewable and recyclable products and made from wood grown in sustainable forests. The logging and manufacturing processes are expected to conform to the environmental regulations of the country of origin.

Hodder & Stoughton Ltd

338 Euston Road

London NW1 3BH

www.hodder.co.uk

Contents

About the author

Hi, and welcome!

I was born in Seoul, Korea, in 1961, and lived in Korea until 1989. In 1989, I first came to the UK to teach Korean language at the School of Oriental and African Studies (SOAS), University of London. I received my B.A. and M.A. in Linguistics at Seoul National University in Korea and Ph.D. in Linguistics at SOAS, University of London. Currently, I am Professor of Korean language and linguistics at SOAS, University of London. I live in Surbiton, Surrey with my wife and two daughters.

I have been teaching Korean at SOAS since 1989 and have taught many European students in the process. They find Korean very difficult, but interesting and hugely rewarding when they make it to the end. This is an introductory Korean course that has been designed for complete beginners. The aim of the book is to make readers learn and talk actual Korean in an easy and stimulating way. While writing the book, I have benefitted enormously from the help of my daughter, Eo-Jin, to whom I would like to express my heartfelt thanks. The book is a collaboration despite the credited single authorship. We have provided readers with easy-to-understand explanations of grammar and as many tips and useful practices as possible.

I have published several books on Korean language learning and Korean grammar over the years. My other publications include: *Korean Grammatical Constructions: Their Form and Meaning* (author, Saffron Books, London), *Korean: A Comprehensive Grammar* (co-author, Routledge), *Elementary Korean and Continuing Korean* (co-author, Tuttle Publishing Co), *Integrated Korean: Advanced I, II* (co-author, University of Hawaii Press) and *Teach Yourself Complete Korean* (co-author, Hodder Education).

Enjoy!

Jaehoon Yeon

How this book works

Welcome to *Get started in Korean*, a course designed for complete beginners! Korean is a fascinating language to study and quite unique, with a completely different alphabet, a grammar structure entirely different to English and sounds unlike any of those of the common European languages. Learning Korean may seem difficult at first but you mustn't be put off. Keep going and you will quickly begin to spot the patterns and understand how things work. Unlike other Asian languages Korean has a phonetic alphabet system that can be learned entirely in six hours and has no confusing tones to cause pronunciation problems.

Each unit in *Get Started in Korean* is structured in the following way:

▶ **What you will learn** identifies what you will be able to do in Korean by the end of the unit.
▶ **Culture point** presents an interesting cultural aspect related to the unit theme, introduces some key words and phrases and includes a challenging question for you.
▶ **Vocabulary builder** introduces key unit vocabulary grouped by theme and conversations, and is accompanied by audio. Learn these words and you will be on your way to speaking fluent Korean.
▶ **Conversations** are recorded dialogues you can listen to and practice, beginning with a narrative that helps you understand what you will hear, a focusing question and follow-up activities.
▶ **Language discovery** draws your attention to key language points in the conversations, whether it is a grammar rule or a way of saying things. Read the notes and look at the conversations to see how the language is used in practice and to aid quicker learning.
▶ **Practice** offers a variety of exercises, including speaking opportunities, to give you a chance to 'pull it all together' and make active use of the language.
▶ **Speaking and listening** offers copious practice in speaking and understanding Korean through exercises that let you use what you have learned in the unit and previously. Try to do the **Speaking** activity spontaneously. The **Listening** activities increase your understanding of spoken Korean. Most exercises include dialogues which appear on the audio but not on the page, so tune up your ears!

- ▶ **Reading and writing** provides practice in reading everyday items and contains mostly vocabulary from the unit. Try getting the gist of the text before you answer the follow-up questions. The passages are often models for personalized writing and completing writing exercises.
- ▶ **Test yourself** helps you assess what you have learned. Do the tests without looking at the text.
- ▶ **Self check** lets you see what you can do in Korean after mastering each unit. When you feel confident that you can use the language correctly, move on to the next unit.

Study the units at your own pace, and remember to make frequent and repeated use of the audio.

To help you through the course, a system of icons indicates the actions you should take

Listen to audio

Speak – speak Korean out loud (even if you're alone)

Figure something out

Culture tip

Exercises coming up!

Reading passage

Write and make notes

Check your Korean ability (no cheating!)

As you work your way through the course, you will also become familiar with studying on your own, looking things up, and checking your Korean language ability.

Here are some resources you can always consult:

- ▶ **Useful expressions** provides a quick reference for everyday phrases and numbers.
- ▶ **Pronunciation guide** overviews Korean sounds. We encourage you to practice pronunciation as you begin the course and go over it regularly. You can find the guide in the beginning of the book.

▶ **The Korean writing system – Hangeul** introduces the alphabet and teaches you how to read and write the language. Start with this and don't be afraid to spend some significant time absorbing the information given. Once you have the foundations in place, working steadily through the rest of the book should be smooth running. You can find the introduction also in the beginning of the book.

▶ **Review** units allow you to consolidate what you have learned in previous units. There are three reviews: after Unit 3, after Unit 6, and after Unit 10. Your score will let you know if you are ready to move ahead or if you should go back and refresh your knowledge.

▶ **Answer key** helps you monitor your performance and check your progress. The **Answer key** includes answers to the activities in the main teaching unit and also to those in the review units.

▶ **Korean–English glossary** allows you to quickly access the vocabulary that is presented in the course.

▶ **Transliteration appendix** offers the romanized version of the Korean script for the conversations. By all means use it to help you on your way as you learn the Korean writing system but avoid relying on it to read the language. Instead, constantly practise reading the Korean directly and only refer to the romanization to test your pronunciation.

Additionally, there is a huge pool of online resources easily accessible for beginners to master the Korean alphabet (Hangeul), from official learning sites hosted by the Korea Tourism Organization to personal video blogs posted on YouTube. Browse around and combine them into your learning with this course! Soon you will be speaking Korean fluently – a language spoken by 80 or 90 million other people, the language of the only nation on Earth still divided, of a country with one of the world's strongest economies and a rich, diverse culture still largely unknown in the West. You will find it both entertaining and fulfilling. So, good luck and have fun! 화이팅!

Learn to learn

The Discovery method

There are lots of approaches to language learning, some practical, some quite unconventional. Perhaps you know of a few, or even have some techniques of your own. In this book we have incorporated the **Discovery method** of learning, a sort of DIY approach to language learning. What this means is that you will be encouraged throughout the course to engage your mind and figure out the language for yourself, through identifying patterns, understanding grammar concepts, noticing words that are similar to English, and more. This method promotes *language awareness*, a critical skill in acquiring a new language. As a result of your own efforts, you will be able to better retain what you have learned, use it with confidence, and, even better, apply those same skills to continuing to learn the language (or, indeed, another one) on your own after you've finished this book.

Everyone can succeed in learning a language – the key is to know how to learn it. Learning is more than just reading or memorizing grammar and vocabulary. It's about being an active learner, learning in real contexts, and, most importantly, *using* what you've learned in different situations. Simply put, if you **figure something out for yourself**, you're more likely to understand it. And when you use what you've learned, you're more likely to remember it.

And because many of the essential but (let's admit it!) dull details, such as grammar rules, are introduced through the **Discovery method**, you'll have more fun while learning. Soon, the language will start to make sense and you'll be relying on your own intuition to construct original sentences *independently*, not just listening and repeating.

Enjoy yourself!

Tips for success

1 MAKE A HABIT OUT OF LEARNING

Study a little every day, between 20 and 30 minutes if possible, rather than two to three hours in one session. **Give yourself short-term goals**, e.g. work out how long you'll spend on a particular unit and work within the time limit. This will help you to **create a study habit**, much in the same way you would a sport or music. You will need to concentrate, so try to **create an environment conducive to learning** which is calm and quiet and free from distractions. As you study, do not worry about your mistakes or the things you can't remember or understand. Languages settle differently in our brains, but gradually the language will become clearer as your brain starts to make new connections. **Just give yourself enough time** and you will succeed.

2 EXPAND YOUR CONTACT WITH THE LANGUAGE

Listen to the radio, watch television or read online articles and blogs in Korean. Do you have a personal passion or hobby? Does a particular news story interest you? Do you like K-pop and other aspects of Korean culture that are currently riding the Korean Hallyu wave? Try to access information about them in Korean. It's entertaining and you'll become used to a range of writing and speaking styles. In time you'll also find that your vocabulary and language recognition deepen.

3 VOCABULARY

- ▶ Group new words under **generic categories** such as *family members* or *food*; situations in which they occur such as, *for asking directions*: *crossroads, traffic lights, left, right, subway station*; and functions such as *greetings, parting, thanks, apologizing*.
- ▶ Write the words over and over. Keep lists on your smartphone or tablet and remember to switch the keyboard language so you can write in the Korean script, rather than using romanization.
- ▶ Listen to the audio several times and say the words out loud as you hear or read them. Use the romanized versions to test your pronunciation if necessary, but as you progress rely on them less.
- ▶ Cover up English translations and try to remember the meanings. Cover up romanizations and pronounce the words on your own.
- ▶ Create flash cards, drawings and mind maps.

- ▶ Write Korean words on post-its and stick them to objects around your house.
- ▶ Look for patterns in words, for example, adding **mae** to a word means *every*, so **maeil** means *every day*, **maeju** means *every week*, **maedal** means *every month* etc.
- ▶ Associate the words with similar sounding words in English, e.g. **mani**, meaning *a lot*, sounds similar to *many*, whilst **pae**, meaning *pear* in Korean, sounds like its English counterpart *pear* etc.
- ▶ **Experiment with words.** Use words in new contexts and find out if they are correct.

4 GRAMMAR

- ▶ Write your own glossary and add new information and examples as you go along.
- ▶ Experiment with rules. Sit back and reflect on how the rules of Korean compare with your own language or other languages you may speak. Try to find rules and be ready to spot the exceptions. By doing this, you'll remember the rules better and get a feel for the language.
- ▶ Try to find examples of grammar in conversations or other articles.
- ▶ Keep a 'pattern bank' of examples for structures you've learned.
- ▶ Use known vocabulary to practise new grammar structures.
- ▶ When you learn a new verb form, write the conjugation of several different verbs you know that follow the same form, for example, looking at verbs ending in a consonant and in a vowel.

5 PRONUNCIATION

- ▶ Keep a section of your notebook for pronunciation rules and list words that give you trouble. Practise them separately.
- ▶ Repeat all of the conversations, line by line. Listen to yourself and try to mimic what you hear.
- ▶ Record yourself and compare yourself to a native speaker.
- ▶ Study individual sounds, then full words.
- ▶ Don't forget, it's not just about pronouncing letters and words correctly, but using the right intonation. So, when practising, mimic the rising and falling intonation of native speakers.

6 LISTENING AND READING

▶ **Imagine the situation.** Try to imagine the scenes and make educated guesses about the topic and vocabulary – a conversation in a café is likely to be about drinks or food.

▶ **Get the gist.** Concentrate on the main part and don't worry about individual words.

▶ **Guess the meaning of key words.** Use the context and your own experience or knowledge of the topic to guess the sorts of words in a reading passage or dialogue.

7 SPEAKING

Rehearse in the foreign language. Successful learners overcome their inhibitions and get into situations where they must speak, write and listen to the foreign language. Here are some tips:

▶ Hold a conversation with yourself using the conversations of the units as models and the structures you have learned previously.

▶ After you have conducted a transaction with a cashier or waiter in your own language, pretend that you have to do it in Korean, e.g. buying groceries, ordering food, drinks and so on.

▶ Look at objects around you and try to name them in Korean.

▶ Look at people around you and try to describe them in detail.

▶ Try to answer all of the questions in the book out loud.

▶ Say the dialogues out loud then try to replace sentences with ones that are true for you.

▶ Try to role-play different situations in the book.

8 LEARN FROM YOUR ERRORS

▶ Don't let errors interfere with getting your message across. Making errors is part of any normal learning process.

▶ Realize that many errors are not serious. Some types of errors do not affect the meaning: the wrong particle (**-ul** instead of **-lul**), wrong pronunciation (**tal** for **ttal**) or wrong verbal ending (**ieyo** rather than **yeyo**). Concentrate on getting your message across and learn from your mistakes.

9 LEARN TO COPE WITH UNCERTAINTY

▶ **Don't over-use your dictionary.** Don't be tempted to look up every word you don't know. Underline new ones and read the passage several times, concentrating on trying to get the gist of the passage. If after the third time there are still words which prevent you from getting the general meaning of the passage, look them up in the dictionary.

▶ **Don't panic if you don't understand.** Just keep going and try to guess what is being said and keep following the conversation or, if you cannot, isolate the expression or words you haven't understood and have them explained to you.

▶ **Keep talking.** The best way to improve your fluency in the foreign language is to talk every time you have the opportunity to do so: keep the conversations flowing and don't worry about the mistakes. If you get stuck for a particular word, don't let the conversation stop; paraphrase or replace the unknown word with one you do know, even if you have to simplify what you want to say. As a last resort use the word from your own language and pronounce it in the foreign accent.

The Korean writing system: Hangeul

HISTORY AND BACKGROUND

The Korean alphabet is unique among all the writing systems of the world because it is the only known alphabet in the world for which the inventor and creation principles were clearly recorded in an official document.

From ancient times, literacy in Korea had existed only among the ruling classes due to its complexity. Chinese characters known as Hanja (한자) had been borrowed and incorporated into the Korean language with Korean pronunciation.

However in 1443, King Sejong, the fourth king of the Joseon Dynasty created Hangeul (한글), the Korean writing system. Originally called Hunmin Jeongeum (훈민정음), meaning 'the correct sounds for the instruction of the people', Hangeul was created to allow common people illiterate in Hanja to accurately, and easily, read and write the Korean language. The supposed publication date, 9 October 1446, is celebrated as Hangeul Day (한글날) in South Korea.

The modern name Hangeul was coined by Korean linguist Ju Si-Gyeong (주시경) in 1912. 'Han' (한) meant 'great' in archaic Korean, whilst 'Geul' (글) denotes 'script' in Korean. 'Han' can also be understood as the Sino-Korean word for 'Korean': 韓. Therefore Hangeul's meaning is 'Korean script' or 'great script'. In North Korea it is known as Choseongeul (조선글).

Both Koreas use Hangeul as their sole official writing system, with ever-decreasing use of Hanja. South Korean newspapers now only use Hanja as abbreviations or disambiguation of homonyms, words with the same spelling and pronunciation but different meanings.

Hangeul is one of the world's most scientific writing systems and has received worldwide acclaim from countless linguists. As a unique systematized phonetic script, Hangeul can express up to 10,000 sounds. It is perhaps the most outstanding scientific and cultural achievement of the Korean nation.

THE BASICS OF THE KOREAN ALPHABET

The modern alphabet consists of 40 letters: 14 basic consonants, 5 double consonants, 8 basic vowels and 13 complex vowels.

Unlike the Latin or Greek alphabets, the alphabetical order of Hangeul does not mix consonants and vowels. The sequence of consonants and vowels are treated separately.

CONSONANTS

There are 14 basic consonants and 5 double consonants. The double consonants are formed from two of the same basic consonants.

Basic consonants: ㄱ, ㄴ, ㄷ, ㄹ, ㅁ, ㅂ, ㅅ, ㅇ, ㅈ, ㅊ, ㅋ, ㅌ, ㅍ, ㅎ.

Double consonants: ㄲ, ㄸ, ㅃ, ㅆ, ㅉ.

VOWELS

There are 8 basic vowel sounds along with 13 other complex vowel sounds. These complex vowels are combinations of no more than two vowels.

Basic vowels: ㅏ, ㅐ, ㅓ, ㅔ, ㅗ, ㅜ, ㅡ, ㅣ.

Complex vowels: ㅑ, ㅒ, ㅕ, ㅖ, ㅘ, ㅙ, ㅚ, ㅛ, ㅝ, ㅞ, ㅟ, ㅠ, ㅢ.

WRITING KOREAN: SYLLABLE BLOCKS

The Korean script, Hangeul, is indeed an alphabet, but it has one special feature which sets it apart from most others. In English we start writing at the beginning of a word and write a sequence of letters, each one following the next, until we reach the end. Usually (apart from the case of silent letters and other peculiarities) we pronounce each letter in turn in the sequence running from left to right.

Korean, however, instead of writing a string of letters in sequence, writes its letters in syllable blocks. Each block-like shape of letters represent a syllable and each letter inside the block forms a sound. The word for *person* is 사람, romanized as **saram**, and consists of two syllables.

The letters ㅅ and ㅏ make the
syllable block 사 (**sa**), while ㄹ,
ㅏ and ㅁ make the next syllable
람 (**ram**). The picture here shows
an approximation of each of the
Korean sounds contained in the
word. Note that written Korean
doesn't actually draw boxes around
the syllables; this is just for illustrative purposes.

Korean syllables are organized into blocks of letters that have a beginning
consonant, a middle vowel and an optional final consonant. A syllable
block is composed of a minimum of two letters, consisting of at least one
consonant and one vowel.

Also note, if you want to only write a vowel, it must be written with the
consonant ㅇ, which acts as a silent placeholder for the consonant
position. Korean syllables, as previously mentioned, must consist of
at least one consonant and one vowel. If one wants to write just the
vowel ㅏ, they would have to write it as 아 with the consonant ㅇ as a
silent placeholder for the consonant position. An easy way to remember
this is to think of the ㅇ as a zero.

Pronunciation guide

This section provides basic guidelines on how each of the 40 Hangeul letter shapes should most normally be pronounced. Note that there are a few changes between the way that Korean is written and the way that it is pronounced. A couple of the basic sound changes are dealt with in the **Basic rules of pronunciation** that follows, but the majority of irregular pronunciations can be practiced in the main unit lessons.

Vowels

There are eight basic vowel sounds: ㅏ, ㅐ, ㅓ, ㅔ, ㅗ, ㅜ, ㅡ and ㅣ.

Here are the eight basic vowels in syllable-block form with the consonant ㅇ. For each vowel sound we have given an example of an English equivalent as well as how it is represented in the romanization adopted in this book.

Vowel	English parallels	Romanization
ㅏ : 아	**a** as in f**a**ther, c**a**rgo	a
ㅐ : 애	**a** as in c**a**re, b**a**re	ae[1]
ㅓ : 어	**o** as in **o**ften, c**o**t	eo (o[2])
ㅔ : 에	**e** as in b**e**d, s**e**t	e[1]
ㅗ : 오	**o** as in c**o**re, t**o**re	o
ㅜ : 우	**u** as in p**u**ll or **oo** as in m**oo**n	u
ㅡ : 으	**u** as in **u**rgh	eu (u[3])
ㅣ : 이	**ee** as in f**ee**t, sh**ee**p	i

Notes:

[1] Many native Korean speakers don't differentiate between 애 and 에, pronouncing both as a sound somewhere between the two.

[2] This may be simplified to *o* in the given romanization when there is no danger of confusion with other vowels.

[3] This may be simplified to *u* in the given romanization when there is no danger of confusion with other vowels.

Korean also has 13 complex vowel sounds: ㅑ, ㅒ, ㅕ, ㅖ, ㅘ, ㅙ, ㅚ, ㅛ, ㅝ, ㅞ, ㅟ, ㅠ and ㅢ. These can be divided into two groups depending on how they are formed and how they sound.

The first is the y-vowels group: ㅑ, ㅒ, ㅕ, ㅖ, ㅛ and ㅠ. These are derived from six of the basic vowel sounds with an additional short stroke and consist of a y-like sound. Here they are written in syllable-block form with English parallels and romanization representation.

Vowel	English parallels	Romanization
ㅑ: 야	**ya** as in **ya**k, **ya**hoo	ya
ㅒ: 얘	**ya** as in **ya**y	yae[1]
ㅕ: 여	**yo** as in **yo**b, **yo**ghurt	yeo (yo[2])
ㅖ: 예	**ye** as in **ye**t, **ye**s	ye[1]
ㅛ: 요	**yo** as in **yo**rk or **yaw** as in **yaw**n	yo
ㅠ: 유	**you** as in **you**, **you**th	yu

Notes:

[1] Many native Korean speakers don't differentiate between 애 and 에, pronouncing both as a sound somewhere between the two.

[2] This may be simplified to *yo* in the given romanization when there is no danger of confusion with other vowels.

The second group of complex vowels is the w-vowels group: ㅘ, ㅙ, ㅚ, ㅝ, ㅞ and ㅟ. These are formed by combining two basic vowels together and consist of a w-like sound. Here they are written in syllable-block form with English parallels and romanization representation.

Vowel	English parallels	Romanization
ㅘ: 와	**wa** as in **wa**x, **wa**g	wa
ㅙ: 왜	**wea** as in **wea**r, **wea**ther	wae[1]
ㅚ: 외	**we** as in **we**t, **we**d	oe[1]
ㅝ: 워	**wo** as in **wo**nder, **wo**n	wo
ㅞ: 웨	**we** as in **we**t, **we**d	we[1]
ㅟ: 위	**wee** as in **wee**p or **wi** as in t**wi**g	wi

Notes:

[1] Many native Korean speakers don't differentiate between 왜, 외 and 웨, pronouncing them as the same sound. The difference in romanization is purely to help you, the learner, differentiate them in terms of spelling.

The final vowel is ㅢ. This complex vowel is a combination of basic vowels ㅡ and ㅣ and is pronounced as a quick glide from 으 [eu] to 이 [i].

Here are all 21 vowels again, listed in the order they'd appear in the dictionary:

Vowel	English parallels	Romanization
ㅏ : 아	**a** as in f**a**ther, c**a**rgo	a
ㅐ : 애	**a** as in c**a**re, b**a**re	ae
ㅑ : 야	**ya** as in **ya**k, **ya**hoo	ya
ㅒ : 얘	**ya** as in **ya**y	yae
ㅓ : 어	**o** as in **o**ften, c**o**t	eo (o)
ㅔ : 에	**e** as in b**e**d, s**e**t	e
ㅕ : 여	**yo** as in **yo**b, **yo**ghurt	yeo (yo)
ㅖ : 예	**ye** as in **ye**t, **ye**s	ye
ㅗ : 오	**o** as in c**o**re, t**o**re	o
ㅘ: 와	**wa** as in **wa**x, **wa**g	wa
ㅙ: 왜	**wea** as in **wea**r, **wea**ther	wae
ㅚ: 외	**we** as in **we**t, **we**d	oe
ㅛ: 요	**yo** as in **yo**rk or **yaw** as in **yaw**n	yo
ㅜ : 우	**u** as in p**u**ll or **oo** as in m**oo**n	u
ㅝ: 워	**wo** as in **wo**nder, **wo**n	wo
ㅞ: 웨	**we** as in **we**t, **we**d	we
ㅟ: 위	**wee** as in **wee**p or **wi** as in tw**i**g	wi
ㅠ: 유	**you** as in **you**, **you**th	yu
ㅡ: 으	**u** as in **u**rgh	eu (u)
ㅢ: 의	**u** (으) followed by **i** (이)	ui
ㅣ : 이	**ee** as in f**ee**t, sh**ee**p	i

<u>00.01</u> **Read through the 21 vowels and try pronouncing them yourself. Then listen to the audio carefully and pronounce each sound as accurately as possible.**

Consonants

There are 14 basic consonants: ㄱ, ㄴ, ㄷ, ㄹ, ㅁ, ㅂ, ㅅ, ㅇ, ㅈ, ㅊ, ㅋ, ㅌ, ㅍ and ㅎ.

Here are the 14 basic consonants in syllable-block form with the vowel ㅏ. For each consonant sound we have given an example of an English equivalent, as well as how it is represented in the romanization adopted in this book.

Consonant	English parallels	Romanization
ㄱ: 가	**k** as in **k**ill or **g** as in a**g**ain	k, g[1]
ㄴ: 나	**n** as in **n**et, **n**ow	n
ㄷ: 다	**t** as in **t**all or **d** as in i**d**ea	t, d[1]
ㄹ: 라	**r** as in **r**ock or **l** as in **l**et, **l**ip	r, l[4]
ㅁ: 마	**m** as in **m**other, **m**arry	m
ㅂ: 바	**p** as in **p**ark or **b** as in a**b**out	p, b[1]

Consonant	English parallels	Romanization
ㅅ: 사	**s** as in **s**ound, **s**ky or **sh** as in **sh**in	s, sh[2]
ㅇ: 아	**ng** as in si**ng**, so**ng**	ng[3]
ㅈ: 자	**j** as in in**j**ury	j
ㅊ: 차	**ch** as in **ch**at, **ch**irp	ch
ㅋ: 카	**k** as in **k**ill, **k**ite	k[h]
ㅌ: 타	**t** as in **t**alk, **t**ake	t[h]
ㅍ: 파	**p** as in **p**ark, **p**rint	p[h]
ㅎ: 하	**h** as in **h**ack, **h**ope	h

Notes:

[1] These three consonants make a different sound, depending on their surrounding letters. The primary pronunciation is a *k*, *t* and *p* sound, but when the consonant has a vowel before and after, its pronunciation changes to a *g*, *d* and *b* sound respectively. This seems complicated but it is an automatic process that comes naturally when talking. In fact in Korean, there are no distinctions between the sounds *k-g*, *t-d* and *p-b*.

[2] The consonant ㅅ is primarily pronounced with an *s*-sound. However, when it comes before the vowel ㅣ, ㅟ or any y-vowel, it becomes a *sh*-sound.

[3] The consonant ㅇ, when at the start of a syllable, is not pronounced; it is a silent consonant. However, when it appears as the final consonant in the syllable it is pronounced as *ng*.

[4] The sounds *l* and *r* cannot be differentiated in Korean. In terms of pronunciation, ㄹ is normally pronounced as *r*, but when it is the final consonant it is pronounced as *l*.

Korean also has five double consonants: ㄲ, ㄸ, ㅃ, ㅆ and ㅉ.

Double consonants are formed of two of the same consonant. They have no close English parallels and are rather similar to Italian double consonants (pp, tt, cc ...). Here they are written in syllable-block form with the vowel ㅏ and romanization representation.

Consonant	English parallels	Romanization
ㄲ: 까	**k** as in s**k**y	kk
ㄸ: 따	**t** as in s**t**yle	tt
ㅃ: 빠	**p** as in s**p**y	pp
ㅆ: 싸	**ss** as in ma**ss s**uicide	ss
ㅉ: 짜	**tch** as in ma**tch**ing	jj

Here are all 19 consonants again, listed in the order they'd appear in the dictionary:

Consonant	English parallels	Romanization
ㄱ: 가	**k** as in **k**ill or **g** as in a**g**ain	k, g
ㄲ: 까	**k** as in s**k**y	kk
ㄴ: 나	**n** as in **n**et, **n**ow	n
ㄷ: 다	**t** as in **t**all or **d** as in i**d**ea	t, d
ㄸ: 따	**t** as in s**t**yle	tt
ㄹ: 라	**r** as in **r**ock or **l** as in **l**et, **l**ip	r, l
ㅁ: 마	**m** as in **m**other, **m**arry	m
ㅂ: 바	**p** as in **p**ark or **b** as in a**b**out	p, b
ㅃ: 빠	**p** as in s**p**y	pp
ㅅ: 사	**s** as in **s**ound, **s**ky or **sh** as in **sh**in	s, sh
ㅆ: 싸	**ss** as in ma**ss** **s**uicide	ss
ㅇ: 아	**ng** as in si**ng**, so**ng**	ng
ㅈ: 자	**j** as in in**j**ury	j
ㅉ: 짜	**tch** as in ma**tch**ing	jj
ㅊ: 차	**ch** as in **ch**at, **ch**irp	ch
ㅋ: 카	**k** as in **k**ill, **k**ite	k^h
ㅌ: 타	**t** as in **t**alk, **t**ake	t^h
ㅍ: 파	**p** as in **p**ark, **p**rint	p^h
ㅎ: 하	**h** as in **h**ack, **h**ope	h

00.02 **Read through the 19 consonants and try pronouncing them yourself. Then listen to the audio carefully and pronounce each sound as accurately as possible.**

00.03 **Using the vowel and consonant tables given, try pronouncing the following words. Listen to the audio to check your pronunciation, and then repeat again to practise.**

These first 12 words have syllables consisting of a single consonant and a single vowel only.

1 바보 *Bapo*
2 바지 *Baji*
3 자주 *Jaju*
4 아이 *ahe*
5 고교 *kogyu*
6 아버지 *ahbeoji*
7 어머니 *eomeoni*
8 가구 *gahgu*
9 두부 *dubu*
10 거기 *geogi*
11 모자 *mojah*
12 모기 *mogi*

These next 12 words include syllables with final consonants.

13 선생님 *Seonsaenim*
14 빵 *bbang*
15 오징어 *ojingeo*
16 영국 *yeonguk*
17 과일 *kaoil*
18 신발 *Sinbal*
19 책 *chaeg*
20 농구 *nongku*
21 사람 *salam*
22 점심 *Jeomsim*
23 저녁 *Jeonyeon*
24 아침 *ahchim*

These last 12 words are English loan words written in Hangeul. Can you guess what they are in English?

25	호텔 *hotel*	**29**	레몬 *lemon*	**33**	오렌지 주스 *orange juice*
26	컴퓨터 *Computer*	**30**	아이스크림 *Ice cream*	**34**	토마토 *tomato*
27	텔레비전 *television*	**31**	햄버거 *hamburger*	**35**	테니스 *tennis*
28	택시 *tense*	**32**	샌드위치 *Sandwich*	**36**	카메라 *camera*

Basic rules of pronunciation

Korean pronunciation is simple and consistent in the sense that all letters correspond to only one sound. This means that once you are familiar with the alphabet, reading Korean is really quite straightforward. Whereas the letter *a* in English could represent various sounds depending on the context and neighbouring letters, the vowel ㅏ in Korean is always pronounced as *a* in *father*, regardless of context and spelling.

In this way Korean writing is consistent. However, some syllables are pronounced in different ways depending on context. The romanized texts in this book will help you pronounce the correct sound changes, but here, outlined below, are a few basic pronunciation rules to help you recognize them.

RULE 1 FINAL CONSONANT SOUNDS

In Korean, the final consonant sound is never distinctly pronounced. We say the last consonant isn't released. This means you say the word as you would in English, shaping your mouth to make the final consonant sound and beginning to say it, but stopping short of releasing any air. Simply put, you slightly mute the consonant sound to sound as if the consonant has been swallowed.

However when the syllable is followed by a vowel, this final consonant sound is released and distinctly pronounced. This final consonant sound is carried over to the initial consonant position of the following syllable, as we've learned that all syllables must start with a consonant.

00.04 Listen carefully to the following examples and practise the pronunciation. Can you hear the consonant sounds being released when followed by the vowels?

1	집	**jip**	집에	**ji-be**
2	앞	**ap**	앞에	**a-pʰe**
3	낮	**nat**	낮에	**na-je**
4	옷	**ot**	옷이	**o-shi**
5	국	**kuk**	국이	**ku-gi**
6	밖	**pak**	밖에	**pa-kke**
7	밭	**pat**	밭에	**pa-tʰe**
8	꽃	**kkot**	꽃이	**kko-chi**

RULE 2 NASALIZATION

When the consonants ㄱ, ㄷ and ㅂ precede the consonants ㅁ or ㄴ, they are pronounced as *ng*, *n* and *m* respectively instead of the standard *k*, *t* and *p*. This process is nasalization. Look at the examples below.

학년 (**hak-nyon**) is pronounced as 항년 to give romanization of **hang-nyon**.

닫는다 (**tat-nun-da**) is pronounced as 단는다 to give romanization of **tan-nun-da**.

합니다 (**hap-ni-da**) is pronounced as 함니다 to give romanization of **ham-ni-da**.

This sounds complex but it is an automatic process that comes naturally when talking so don't worry about it too much. You will get used to it as you learn more throughout the course.

00.05 Listen to the additional examples and practise the pronunciation.

1	먹는다	(**mok-nun-da**)	멍는다	**mong-nun-da**
2	한국말	(**han-guk-mal**)	항궁말	**hang-gung-mal**
3	걷는다	(**kot-nun-da**)	건는다	**kon-nun-da**
4	받는다	(**pat-nun-da**)	반는다	**ban-nun-da**
5	갑니다	(**kap-ni-da**)	감니다	**kam-ni-da**
6	십만	(**ship-man**)	심만	**shim-man**

Didn't know
Did know

Useful expressions

GREETINGS, FAREWELLS AND COURTESIES

hello	안녕하세요	**annyong haseyo**
goodbye	안녕히 가세요	**annyonghi kaseyo**
see you later	또 만나요	**tto mannayo**
see you tomorrow	내일 또 만나요	**naeil tto mannayo**
how are you?	안녕하세요?	**annyong haseyo?**
yes	네/예	**ne/ye**
no	아니요	**aniyo**
please	부탁합니다	**put^{h}ak^{h}amnida**
thank you	고맙습니다	**komapsumnida**
	감사합니다	**kamsahamnida**
you're welcome (it's OK)	괜찮아요.	**kwenchanayo**
excuse me	실례합니다	**sillehamnida**
sorry	미안합니다	**mian hamnida**
	죄송합니다	**joesong hamnida**

MAKING YOURSELF UNDERSTOOD

please repeat that	다시 말해주세요	**tashi malhae juseyo**
please speak slowly	천천히 말해주세요	**chonchoni malhae juseyo**
I don't understand	모르겠어요	**morugessoyo**
I understand	알겠어요	**algessoyo**
I don't speak Korean	한국말 못해요	**hanggungmal mot^{h}aeyo**

QUESTION WORDS

where?	어디?	**odi?**
how?	어떻게?	**ottokʰe?**
when?	언제?	**onje?**
how much?	얼마?	**olma?**
why?	왜?	**wae?**
who?	누구?	**nugu?**

NUMBERS

There are two number systems in Korean: a Korean set called pure Korean numbers, and another of Chinese origin called Sino-Korean numbers. Numbers are used for counting things, and which set you use in any situation depends on what it is you want to count! You just have to learn which numbers are used with which counters – there's no shortcut I'm afraid!

Both number systems follow very logical patterns.

Pure Korean numbers

The pure Korean system tends to be used for smaller, more common numbers. In fact, there are no pure Korean numbers above 99! Common counters that use pure Korean numbers include years of age, number of items such as bottles or books, and the number of hours when indicating the duration of something.

00.06 **Listen to the audio for the pronunciation of these Pure Korean numbers.**

1	하나	**hana**	11	열하나	**yolhana**	10	열	**yol**
2	둘	**tul**	12	열둘	**yoltul**	20	스물	**sumul**
3	셋	**set**	13	열셋	**yolset**	30	서른	**sorun**
4	넷	**net**	14	열넷	**yolnet**	40	마흔	**mahun**
5	다섯	**tasot**	15	열다섯	**yoltasot**	50	쉰	**swin**
6	여섯	**yosot**	16	열여섯	**yolyosot**	60	예순	**yesun**
7	일곱	**ilgop**	17	열일곱	**yolilgop**	70	일흔	**ilhun**
8	여덟	**yodol**	18	열여덟	**yolyodol**	80	여든	**yodun**
9	아홉	**ahop**	19	열아홉	**yolahop**	90	아흔	**ahun**
10	열	**yol**	20	스물	**sumul**	100	백	**paek**

Numbers 11 through 99 are represented by combining the 'tens' and 'ones'. For example, 11 is formed by combining 10 (열) and 5 (다섯) to give 열다섯. Similarly, 21 is formed by combining 20 (스물) and 1 (하나) to give 스물하나.

Sino-Korean numbers

Common counters that use Sino-Korean numbers include minutes and money. Sino-Korean numbers are also used to state the date.

 00.07 Listen to the audio for the pronunciation of these Sino-Korean numbers.

1 일	il	11 십일	shibil	10 십	ship
2 이	i	12 십이	shibi	20 이십	iship
3 삼	sam	13 십삼	shipsam	30 삼십	samship
4 사	sa	14 십사	shipsa	40 사십	saship
5 오	o	15 십오	shibo	50 오십	oship
6 육	yuk	16 십육	shimnyuk	60 육십	yukship
7 칠	chil	17 십칠	shipchil	70 칠십	chilship
8 팔	pʰal	18 십팔	shipʰal	80 팔십	pʰalship
9 구	ku	19 십구	shipku	90 구십	kuship
10 십	ship	20 이십	iship	100 백	paek
100 백	paek	600 육백	yukpaek	1000 천	chon
200 이백	ibaek	700 칠백	chilpaek	10000 만	man
300 삼백	sambaek	800 팔백	pʰalpaek	100000 십만	shimman
400 사백	sabaek	900 구백	kubaek	1000000 백만	paengman
500 오백	obaek	1000 천	chon		

Numbers between 11 and 99 are formed by combining the 'tens' and 'ones'. One step simpler than the pure Korean numbers, the words for 20 to 90 are in fact the relevant tens digit and 'ten' combined.

The number 20 is 'two-ten', so 이십, 30 is 'three-ten' so 삼십 and so on. It is the same pattern for the hundreds, thousands and much larger units. Therefore, once you know the words for each unit it becomes very simple to count up to huge numbers.

A more complicated example is the number 3895. Think of it as 'three-thousand, eight-hundred, nine-tens, and five' which gives you 삼천팔백구십오 in Korean.

안녕하세요! 저는 영국사람이에요.

Hello! I'm British.

In this unit, you will learn how to:
▶ *say hello and goodbye.*
▶ *exchange greetings.*
▶ *introduce yourself.*
▶ *ask people about themselves.*

CEFR: *(A1) Can make an introduction by asking and answering questions about personal details such as one's name, occupation and nationality. (A1) Can exchange and understand basic greeting and leave-taking expressions.*

📷 Greeting, bowing and names

Koreans greet each other with 안녕하세요 **annyonghaseyo** and bid farewell with 안녕히 가세요 **annyonghi kaseyo**. 안녕하세요 simultaneously carries the meaning *Hello* and *How are you?*, to which people reply 안녕하세요 again. They usually bow their heads when greeting, especially if they are greeting a person of higher status whether socially or with regard to age. Today, many people also greet each other with a 악수 **aksu** (*handshake*), and in the workplace, business people exchange their 명함 **myongham** (*namecard*) upon meeting as a form of self-introduction.

You may have noticed that personal names mostly consist of three syllables: the first is the 성 **seong** (*surname*), which is then followed by the 이름 **irum** (*first name*), normally consisting of two syllables. The surname always comes first. When addressing someone you should use the polite title -씨 **-ssi** after the first name. You may choose to use the full name followed by -씨 **-ssi** to create a sense of formality for first meetings.

How would you expect a Korean to greet and address you when you meet for the first time?

Vocabulary builder

01.01 **Read the vocabulary and try to pronounce each word. Then listen and try to imitate the speakers.**

NATIONALITIES AND OCCUPATIONS

> **NATIONALITIES**
> To state nationality, give the country's name with the word 사람 (**saram**), meaning *person*. For example, *America* is 미국 (**miguk**); *American* is 미국 사람 (**miguk saram**).

한국 사람	hangguk saram	*Korean (person)*
영국 사람	yongguk saram	*British (person)*
미국 사람	miguk saram	*American (person)*
중국 사람	jungguk saram	*Chinese (person)*
호주 사람	hoju saram	*Australian (person)*
일본 사람	ilbon saram	*Japanese (person)*
선생	sonsaeng	*teacher*
회사원	hwesawon	*office worker*
의사	uisa	*doctor*
주부	jubu	*housewife*
요리사	yorisa	*chef*
변호사	pyonhosa	*lawyer*

NEW EXPRESSIONS

안녕하세요!	Annyonghaseyo!	*Hello!/How are you?*
안녕히 가세요!	Annyonghi kaseyo!	*Goodbye!*
만나서 반가워요.	Mannaso pangawoyo.	*Nice to meet you.*
다음에 또 봐요.	Taume tto pwayo.	*See you again next time.*
저는 . . . 이에요/예요.	Jonun . . . ieyo/yeyo.	*I am . . .*
어느 나라 사람이에요?	Onu nara saramieyo?	*What nationality are you?*
직업이 뭐예요?	Jigobi mwoyeyo?	*What is your occupation?*

💡 Conservations

<u>01.02</u> *Two male students are meeting for the first time. Listen and answer the question.*

lee cheol so
Kim Sangmin

1 What are the students' names?

학생 1	안녕하세요. 저는 이철수예요. ✔ *cheol so*
학생 2	안녕하세요. 저는 김상민이에요. ✔ *sangmin*
학생 1	상민씨, 만나서 반가워요.
학생 2	철수씨, 만나서 반가워요.
학생 1	다음에 또 봐요. 안녕히 가세요.
학생 2	안녕히 가세요.

<u>01.03</u> *A lady has joined a fitness group and is introducing herself to the class. Listen and answer the questions.*

2 What is the lady's name? *choi hanbyeol*

여자	안녕하세요. 저는 최한별이에요. ✔
모두	한별씨, 안녕하세요.
여자	저는 한국 사람이에요. 저는 의사예요. 만나서 반가워요.
모두	만나서 반가워요.

3 Read or listen to the conversation again and answer these questions.

　a What is the lady's nationality? *korean* ✔
　b What is the lady's occupation? *doctor* ✔

4 Find the expressions in the conversation that mean:

✔**a** Hello. I am Hanbyol Choi.　**d** - 만나서 반가워요
✔**b** I am Korean.　　　　　　　*mannaseo bangawoyo*
✔**c** I am a doctor.
✔**d** Nice to meet you.

a. 안녕하세요 저는 최한별이에요
annyeonghaseyo jeonun choi hanbyeol eyie

b. 저는 한국 사람이에요
jeonun hangeuk saram ieyo

c. 저는 의사예요
jeonun eusa yeyo

4

<u>01.04</u> *The lady is paired with Jimmy Smith in the fitness class. Listen to their conversation and answer the questions.*

5 Have the lady and Jimmy met before?

여자	안녕하세요. 만나서 반가워요. 저는 최한별이에요.
지미 스미스	안녕하세요. 저는 지미 스미스예요. 만나서 반가워요.
여자	지미씨, 어느 나라 사람이에요?
지미 스미스	저는 미국 사람이에요.
여자	직업은 뭐예요?
지미 스미스	저는 선생이에요.

6 Read or listen to the conversation again and answer these questions.

   a What is Jimmy's nationality?

   b What is Jimmy's occupation?

7 Find the expressions in the conversation that mean:

   a I am Jimmy Smith.

   b What nationality are you?

   c I am American.

   d What is your occupation?

   e I am a teacher.

8 Try to remember the words then complete the sentences.

   a 저는 지미 스미스 _____. 만나서 _____.

   b 지미씨, _____ _____ 사람이에요?

   c 저는 한국 _____ 이에요.

   d _____ 은 뭐예요?

   e 저는 선생 _____.

9 <u>01.05</u> Now imagine you are the lady's partner. Listen to the English prompts and answer her questions with your own information.

Language discovery

 Find these sentences in the last conversation. Can you figure out what the Korean for _I am . . ._ is?

　　a I am a teacher.
　　b I am an American.

1 VERBS AND VERB ENDINGS

In Korean, sentences always end with the verb, a 'doing-word' such as _talk_ or _go_. The main verbs always come at the end, and getting used to this major difference in sentence structure can take a little time.

Verbs are made up of stems onto which endings are added. Every verb has a stem; it is the most basic part of the verb. The stem indicates the meaning of the word, and the various endings can indicate everything from the style of speech (depending on who you are talking to) to which tense you are speaking in (past, present, or future, for example).

Korean has various styles or levels of speech used according to social situation. For example, when you are having a drink with close friends, you speak in a very different style from that which you would use if you were addressing a meeting or talking to somebody for the first time. Although we have formal and informal language in English, we do not have anything as systematic and widespread as the Korean system of verb endings. In Korean, these verb endings are crucial to every sentence, since you cannot say a sentence without selecting a speech style in which to say it!

Verbs are presented in -다 **-ta** form in the dictionary; that is, they all end with the letters -다. The verb with this -다 removed simply becomes the verb stem, to which we add the appropriate endings when necessary. As with all languages, there are irregular verbs in Korean where stems can contract or combine with certain endings to look different from the original stem. All expressions introduced throughout this book are given in full and don't require you to work out any verb endings independently. A detailed introduction to conjugating verbs in various tenses is given in the latter units.

2 THE POLITE ENDING: -요 YO

What is the most important verb ending? The polite style ending -요 **yo**. It is the most common way of ending sentences in everyday conversation. -요 can be used in most social situations, which are neither very formal nor intimate. In other words, -요 is the middle-of-the-road style.

3 THE COPULA: 'TO BE'

The main verb introduced in Unit 1 is the copula -이다 **-ida**. You use this special form to say that something is something else (e.g. *He is a teacher*). Like all other Korean verbs, the copula comes at the end of the sentence. When attached to a noun the copula functions like the verb *to be* in English.

Using the polite style ending -요 **-yo**, it can take these two forms: -이에요 **-ieyo** and -예요 **-yeyo**. Some sentences can end with -이에요 and others with -예요, depending on the preceding noun's endings:

▶ If the previous noun ends in a consonant, -이에요 follows:

저는 한국 사람이에요.   **Jonun hanguk saram ieyo.**   *I am Korean.*

▶ If the previous noun ends in a vowel, -예요 follows:

저는 의사예요.   **Jonun uisa yeyo.**   *I am a doctor.*

*Is in this sense means *is equivalent to, is identical with*; but it does not mean *is located in* or *is a certain way*. English makes no distinction but Korean does, so watch out!

4 FORMATION: 'I AM', 'SHE IS', 'JIMMY IS'

The phrase 저는 . . . -이에요/예요 **Jonun . . . -ieyo/yeyo** translates into *I am . . .* in English. To say *she is . . . , they are . . .* or perhaps *Jimmy is . . .* you simply replace 저는 **Jonun** with the appropriate pronoun or name. See Unit 2 for more information.

C3. haume HO puayo

 Practice

1 These phrases use the polite style ending -요. Match the phrases and translations.

a 안녕하세요.
b 만나서 반가워요.
c 다음에 또 봐요.
d 안녕히 가세요.

1 Hello. How are you?
2 Goodbye.
3 Nice to meet you.
4 See you again next time.

2 01.06 Answer the following. Say your answers out loud then listen and check your answers.

a Ask what nationality Sarah is. Address the question to Sarah.
b Ask Matthew what his occupation is. Address the question to Matthew.
c Say that you are English.
d Say that you are a teacher.
e Ask Jimin what nationality she is. Address the question to Jimin. Then give her answer as if she is Korean.
f Ask Youngmin what his occupation is. Address the question to Youngmin then give his answer as if he is a doctor.

3 Complete the sentences with the correct verb ending of the copula -이다. Note the final letter of the preceding noun.

a 저는 태국 사람   ...(이에요/예요)
b 저는 독일 사람   ...(이에요/예요)
c 저는 프랑스 사람   ...(이에요/예요)
d 저는 교수   ...(이에요/예요)
e 저는 공무원   ...(이에요/예요)
f 저는 치과 의사   ...(이에요/예요)
g 저는 변호사   ...(이에요/예요)

Speaking

Complete the conversation with answers that are true for you. Use the English prompts to help you.

Jimin	안녕하세요!
You	*Say 'Hello'.*
Jimin	저는 지민이에요.
You	*Say your name. Then say 'Nice to meet you'.*
Jimin	만나서 반가워요. 직업이 뭐예요?
You	*Tell her your occupation. Then ask what her occupation is. Address the question to Jimin.*
Jimin	저는 요리사예요.
You	*Ask her what nationality she is. Tell her your nationality.*
Jimin	저는 한국 사람이에요.
You	*Say 'See you again next time, goodbye'.*
Jimin	안녕히 가세요!

Listening

1 <u>01.07</u> **Listen to the conversation and fill in the missing details.**

Name		Nationality	Occupation
a Person 1 (Male)	**1** _____	**2** _____	**3** _____
b Person 2 (Female)	**1** _____	**2** _____	**3** _____

2 <u>01.08</u> **Listen and choose the correct answer.**

   a Her name is _____ .   (Stephanie/Fiona/Penelope)

   b She is _____ .   (Australian/French/Chinese)

   c She is a _____ .   (doctor/housewife/teacher)

Reading and writing

1 Look at the name card and fili in the following details.

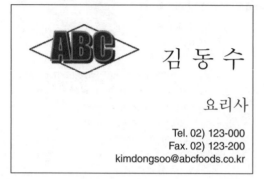

ABC

김 동 수

요리사

Tel. 02) 123-000
Fax. 02) 123-200
kimdongsoo@abcfoods.co.kr

a Name: _____
b Occupation: _____

2 Read the email and complete the details about the penpal.

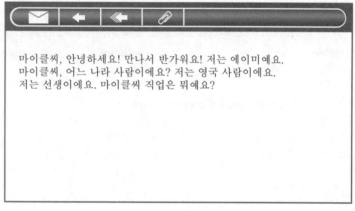

마이클씨, 안녕하세요! 만나서 반가워요! 저는 에이미예요.
마이클씨, 어느 나라 사람이에요? 저는 영국 사람이에요.
저는 선생이에요. 마이클씨 직업은 뭐예요?

a Name: _____
b Nationality: _____
c Occupation: _____

3 Reply to the penpal using the following information:
(Michael/British/Chef).

4 Now, reply to the penpal as yourself using your own details.

Test yourself

1 How would you do the following?

a Say 'Hello. Nice to meet you'.

_____

b Say 'Goodbye. See you again next time'.

_____

c Say your name.

_____

d Say what nationality you are.

_____

e Say what your occupation is.

_____

f Ask someone what his/her nationality is.

_____

g Ask someone what his/her occupation is.

_____

2 Complete these sentences with the correct form of the copula -이다.

a 저는 중국 사람 _____.　　**d** 저는 의사_____.
b 저는 러시아 사람_____.　　**e** 저는 학생_____.
c 저는 공무원_____.　　**f** 저는 요리사_____.

SELF CHECK

I CAN . . .
. . . say hello and goodbye.
. . . tell someone my name.
. . . tell someone my nationality.
. . . tell someone my occupation.
. . . ask others about themselves.

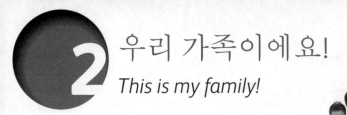

2

우리 가족이에요!

This is my family!

In this unit, you will learn how to:
▶ *say how many people there are in your family.*
▶ *introduce members of your family.*
▶ *say your age, as well as the age of others.*
▶ *ask others about their families.*

CEFR: *(A2) Can understand sentences and frequently used expressions describing relatives by name, age and occupation. (A1) Can deal with numbers to count family members and state people's ages.*

Family values and traditions

Like in many other Asian societies, Confucianism is deeply embedded in Korea's traditional values and culture. Quintessential to Confucianism is respect for elders and seniority, duty, loyalty, honour and candour. This helps explain the numerous honorific (polite) variations of the language that you will begin to learn in this unit.

When Koreans introduce their 가족 **kajok** (*family*), they use the word *our* instead of *my*, so one would say 우리 가족이에요 **uri kajogieyo** (*This is our family*). In the past, most households were a 대가족 **taegajok** (*extended family*), with several generations living together under one roof. A typical family would be headed by the 장남 **jangnam** (*eldest son*) who, with his 아내 **anae** (*wife*), would have full responsibility of his parents' care. Due to these traditionally larger households, terminology used for blood ties and relations through marriage is particularly well developed in Korean. Today, most households are now in the form of a 핵가족 **haekkajok** (*nuclear family*), in which a 부부 **pubu** (*husband and wife*) is the centre of a family.

Which Korean word in **bold** from the text means *our*? If 아내 means *wife*, how would you say *my wife* in Korean?

Vocabulary builder

02.01 **Read the vocabulary and try to pronounce each word. Then listen and try to imitate the speakers.**

FAMILY RELATIONSHIPS

할아버지, 할머니	haraboji, halmoni	*grandfather, grandmother*
아버지, 어머니	aboji, omoni	*father, mother*
형, 누나	hyong, nuna	*boy's older brother/sister*
오빠, 언니	oppa, onni	*girl's older brother/sister*
남동생, 여동생	namdongsaeng, yodongsaeng	*younger brother/sister*
남편, 아내	namphyon, anae	*husband, wife*
아들, 딸	adul, ttal	*son, daughter*

NEW EXPRESSIONS

가족이 몇 명이에요?	Kajogi myon myongieyo?	*How many are in your family?*
누구누구예요?	Nugu nugu yeyo?	*Who are they?*
-하고	-hago	*and*
그리고	kurigo	*and, also*
결혼했어요?	Kyolhon haessoyo?	*Are you married?*
아이 있어요?	Ai issoyo?	*Do you have any children?*
예. / 아니요.	Ye/Anio.	*Yes/No.*
이름이 뭐예요?	Irumi mwoyeyo?	*What is his/her name?*
성함이 어떻게 되세요?	Songhami ottokhe tweseyo?	*What is his/her name? (hon)*
나이가 몇 살이에요?	Naiga myossal ieyo?	*How old is he/she?*
연세가 어떻게 되세요?	Yonsega ottokhe tweseyo?	*How old is he/she? (hon)*

> ### HONORIFIC KOREAN
> Honorific, or polite, variations of Korean are used when speaking to or about social elders to show respect. In addition to adapted verb endings, honorific nouns are sometimes also used. For example 성함 **songham** may be used instead of 이름 **irum**, meaning *name*, and 연세 **yonse** may be used in place of 나이 **nai**, meaning *age*. The abbreviation (hon) indicates an honorific variation.

Conversations

02.02 Junsu is asking Yongho about his family. Listen and answer the questions.

1 Does Yongho live with any grandparents?

준수	용호씨, 가족이 몇 명이에요?
용호	우리 가족은 네명이에요.
준수	누구누구예요?
용호	우리 아버지, 어머니, 여동생하고 저예요.
준수	아버지는 성함이 어떻게 되세요?
용호	최민관이세요. 우리 아버지는 교수세요.
준수	연세가 어떻게 되세요?
용호	마흔두살이세요.
준수	여동생은 이름이 뭐예요? 그리고 나이가 몇 살이에요?
용호	우리 여동생은 최용미예요. 그리고 용미는 열세살이에요.

2 Read or listen to the conversation again and answer these questions.
 a How many people are there in Yongho's family? Who are they?
 b What is Yongho's father called? What is his occupation? How old is he?
 c How is Yongmi related to Yongho? How old is Yongmi?

3 Can you say the following in English?
 a 우리 가족은 네명이에요.
 b 우리 아버지, 어머니, 여동생하고 저예요.
 c 아버지는 성함이 어떻게 되세요?
 d 우리 아버지는 교수세요.
 e 그리고 나이가 몇살이에요?
 f 영미는 열세살이에요.

 4 *02.03 Junsu wants to find out about you and your family. Answer his questions to describe them. Listen carefully as the questions are slightly different. Use the English prompts to help you.*

Jangho bumps into his old high school friend Minjun and introduces him to his wife. Listen and answer the questions.

5 What is Jangho's wife called?

> **EXTRA VOCABULARY**
>
> | 오랜만이에요! | *Long time no see!* |
> |---|---|
> | 인사해요. | *Say hello.* |

장호	민준씨! 오랜만이에요! 인사해요. 우리 아내예요.
수빈	안녕하세요. 저는 최수빈이에요. 만나서 반가워요.
민준	안녕하세요! 저는 박민준이에요.
장호	(*to his wife*) 민준씨는 교수예요. 그리고 서른다섯살이에요.
	(*to Minjun*) 민준씨, 결혼 했어요?
민준	예. 결혼 했어요. 아이 두명 있어요. 딸하고 아들 있어요.

6 Read or listen to the conversation again and answer these questions.
a Who is Subin?
b What is Minjun's occupation? How old is he?
c Is Minjun married? Does he have any children? If so, how many?

7 Can you say the following in Korean?
a Say hello. This is my younger brother.
b Minjun is a lawyer. And he is 29 years old.
c I have three children.

8 Match the questions and answers. Note any honorifics.
a 아이 있어요?
b 아버지는 연세가 어떻게 되세요?
c 어머니는 직업이 어떻게 되세요?
d 언니는 이름이 뭐예요?
e 여동생은 몇 살이에요?

1 우리 언니는 김미진이에요.
2 우리 여동생은 열여섯 살이에요.
3 네. 아이 있어요. 딸 있어요.
4 우리 아버지는 쉰한 살이세요.
5 우리 어머니는 요리사세요.

Language discovery

 Look at the sentences below and find the common syllable -는. Can you guess its function? What do you also notice about the sentence endings?

저는 교수예요.	**Jo nun kyosuyeyo.**
우리 동생 민준이는 열한살이에요.	**Uri tongsaeng minjuni nun yolhansalieyo.**
우리 아버지는 마흔두살이세요.	**Uri aboji nun mahuntusal iseyo.**
우리 어머니는 주부세요.	**Uri omoni nun jubuseyo.**

1 TOPIC PARTICLE: -은/는 -UN/NUN

Korean has a particle which can be attached to a noun or a phrase to emphasize that it is the topic of the sentence, that is to say, it is the thing which is being talked about. Sometimes we do this in English with an expression like *as for* . . . for emphasis. For example, *As for my business, it's going pretty well at the moment*. Korean does this frequently with the topic particle -은/는 **-un/nun**.

▶ If the previous noun ends in a consonant, -은 follows.

우리 여동생은 . . .	**uri yodonsaeng un . . .**	*My younger sister is . . .*

▶ If the previous noun ends in a vowel, -는 follows.

우리 아버지는 . . .	**uri aboji nun . . .**	*My father is . . .*

2 PURE KOREAN NUMBERS AS COUNTERS

As mentioned, *(years of) age* is a common counter that uses pure Korean numbers. When used in such situations as a counter or when followed by a noun, numbers ending with 1, 2, 3 or 4 lose their last letter. For example, notice how *42 years old* is 마흔두살 **mahun tusal**, not 마흔둘살 **mahun tulsal**. The last letter of the word for 2, ㄹ, is removed. For 1, the last letter ㅏ is lost to give 한- **han-**; for 2 the last letter ㄹ is lost to give 두- **tu-**; for 3 and 4, the last letter ㅅ is lost to give 세- **se-** and 네- **ne-**.

3 HONORIFIC SENTENCE ENDINGS: -(이)세요 -(I)SEYO

You will notice many sentences end with -이세요/세요 **-iseyo/seyo** rather than the -이에요/예요 **-ieyo/yeyo** ending learned in Unit 1. One shows respect for elders by using this polite form, as shown in the first conversation between Yongho and Junsu. When Yongho speaks of his parents he uses the honorific ending to say, 마흔두살이세요 **mahuntusal iseyo** rather than 마흔두살이에요 **mahuntusal ieyo**.

Thus this ending is the polite honorific form that honours the person you are talking about and shows respect for the subject of the sentence. The appropriate ending, -이세요 **-iseyo** or 세요 **-seyo**, depends on the final letter of the preceding word.

▶ If the previous noun ends in a consonant, -이세요 follows.

우리 아버지는 마흔두살<u>이세요</u>.   **uri abojinun mahuntusal iseyo.**
My father is 42 years old.

▶ If the previous noun ends in a vowel, -세요 follows.

우리 아버지는 교수<u>세요</u>.   **uri abojinun kyosuseyo.**
My father is a professor.

4 TWO WAYS OF SAYING 'AND'

-하고 **-hago** and 그리고 **kurigo** both mean *and*, but their uses are very different.

▶ -하고 **-hago** is used to join two nouns. For example, when saying *I have a daughter and a son*, you say 딸<u>하고</u> 아들 있어요 **ttal hago adul issoyo**.

▶ 그리고 **kurigo** is used to join two sentences. It is used in a similar fashion to *also* or *in addition* at the beginning of a sentence. For example, when saying *My younger sister is Choi Yongmi. And Yongmi is 13 years old.* you would say 우리 여동생은 최용미예요. <u>그리고</u> 용미는 열세살이에요. **uri yodongsaengun Choi Yongmiyeyo. Kurigo Yongminun yolsesalieyo.**

Beginners in Korean often try joining two sentences with the word 하고 instead of 그리고. One might say 영미는 열세살이에요. <u>하고</u> 우리 여동생은 학생이에요. **Yongminun yolsesal ieyo. Hago uri yodongsaengun haksaeng ieyo.** Though people would understand what you mean, the use sounds childish and is seen as incorrect.

Practice

1 Give these numbers using the pure Korean number system. Then give them as ages. Does the Korean change? Follow the example.

Example: 74 일흔넷   일흔네살 (넷 loses its last letter ㅅ)

a 36   **c** 19   **e** 68   **g** 23

b 84   **d** 75   **f** 41   **h** 52

2 Complete the sentences with the correct topic particle and verb ending of the copula -이다.

  a 우리 가족   (은/는) 모두 다섯명   (이에요/예요/이세요/세요).
  b 우리 아버지 (은/는) 쉰다섯살   (이에요/예요/이세요/세요).
  c 어머니 성함 (은/는) 세라 콜린스   (이에요/예요/이세요/세요).
  d 우리 형   (은/는) 현준   (이에요/예요/이세요/세요).
  e 우리 여동생 (은/는) 학생   (이에요/예요/이세요/세요).
  f 우리 아내   (은/는) 스위스 사람 (이에요/예요/이세요/세요).
  g 우리 딸   (은/는) 열아홉살   (이에요/예요/이세요/세요).
  h 우리 아들   (은/는) 요리사   (이에요/예요/이세요/세요).

3 02.05 Say your answers to the following questions out loud then listen and check your answers.

  a Ask how old Junsu's grandfather is. Address the question to Junsu.
  b Ask what Yongho's mother's name is. Address the question to Yongho.
  c Say your father is 52 years old.
  d Say your younger sister is a housewife.
  e Ask James how old his daughter is. What will he say if she is seven years old?
  f Ask James what his son is called. What will he say if he is called Matthew?

Speaking

Complete the conversation as Junsu. This time Junsu is describing his family to Yongho. Use the English prompts to help you.

Yongho 준수씨, 가족이 몇 명이에요? 누구누구예요?

Junsu *Say there are five people in your family. Your father, mother, older brother, younger sister and yourself.*

Yongho 아버지는 연세가 어떻게 되세요?

Junsu *Say your father is 61 years old.*

Yongho 어머니는 직업이 어떻게 되세요?

Junsu *Say your mother is an office worker.*

Yongho 형은 몇 살이세요? 형은 결혼 했어요?

Junsu *Say your old brother is 33 years old. Then say 'Yes, he is married'. Say he has a daughter.*

Yongho 여동생은 이름이 뭐예요? 그리고 몇 살이에요?

Junsu *Say your younger sister is called Junhee. Also say she is 25 years old.*

Listening

1 <u>02.06</u> Listen to Jumin, Hani and Minjun introduce their families. Match the names and families.

a Jumin   **b** Hani   **c** Minjun

1

2

3

2 <u>02.07</u> Listen to the conversation and answer true or false.

a Kyungsun has three daughters.

b Kyungsun has a daughter called Kyungmin.

c Kyungsun has a ten-year-old daughter called Kyungji.

d Jisok is not married.

e Jisok has a family of three.

f Jisok's son is 12 years old.

Reading and writing

1 Read the passage and answer the questions.

우리 가족은 할아버지, 할머니, 아버지, 어머니,
누나하고 저, 모두 여섯 명이에요. 우리 아버지는
변호사세요. 그리고 우리 어머니는 공무원이세요.
누나는 열여덟살이에요. 우리 누나 이름은 한 정
민이에요. 누나는 대학생이에요. 저는 열네살이에요.
그리고 학생이에요

a How many people are there in this family?
b What do the parents do for a living?
c How many children are there in the family?
d Is the main character male or female? How can you tell?
e Is the main character the eldest or youngest child? How can you tell?
f What is the main character's occupation?

2 Read the passage then fill in the missing details below.

안녕하세요 저는 존이에요. 우리 가족은 모두 네명이에요.
저, 아내, 아들하고 딸, 네 명이에요. 저는 쉰다섯살이에요.
그리고 교수예요. 우리 아내 메리는 쉰한살이에요.
주부예요. 우리 아들은 마이클이에요.
나이는 서른살이에요. 우리 딸 제니퍼는 스물일곱살이에요.
우리 아들은 변호사예요. 그리고 우리 딸은 요리사예요.

Name	Relation	Age	Occupation
John	—	**a** _____	**b** _____
c _____	**d** _____	51	**e** _____
f _____	Son	**g** _____	**h** _____
i _____	**j** _____	**k** _____	Chef

3 Look back at the previous question. Write a similar passage about your own family. Try to describe as many family members as possible, including honorific expressions. Give names, ages and occupations where possible.

Test yourself

1 How would you do the following?

  a Say how many people there are in your family.

  _____

  b Say your parents' occupation and ages.

  _____

  c Name and describe a sibling.

  _____

  d Give the numbers in full using the pure Korean number system.

  58 _____   92 _____   17 _____   34 _____

2 Match the phrases and situations.

a 공무원이세요.	**1**	To ask the name of a sibling.
b 열두살이에요.	**2**	To ask the age of an elder.
c 마흔다섯살이세요.	**3**	To say my age or the age of a sibling.
d 주부예요.	**4**	To say the age of an elder.
e 이름이 뭐예요?	**5**	To say my occupation.
f 나이가 어떻게 되세요?	**6**	To say the occupation of an elder.

3 Complete the sentences using the grammar points learned in this unit.

  a 아버지 _____ 의사 _____.

  b 동생 _____ 학생 _____.

  c 우리 어머니 _____ 마흔세살 _____.

  d 우리 언니 _____ 열다섯살 _____.

SELF CHECK

	I CAN . . .
○	. . . say how many people there are in my family and list them.
○	. . . say how many siblings I have.
○	. . . describe a relative by name, age and occupation.
○	. . . ask others about their families.
○	. . . ask someone if s/he is married and has children.

3 날짜, 시간, 오늘 날씨

Date, time, today's weather

In this unit, you will learn how to:
▶ *say how old you are.*
▶ *say when your birthday is.*
▶ *give the date.*
▶ *say what time it is.*
▶ *describe the weather.*

CEFR: *(A1) Can understand and use basic phrases to describe the date, time and today's weather. (A2) Can deal with numbers using various counters such as years of age, hours and minutes.*

The calendar

The Korean 달력 **tallyok** (*calendar*) is a lunisolar calendar, in which the 날짜 **naljja** (*date*) indicates both the moon phase and the time of the solar year. Though Koreans use the 양력 **yangnyok** (*solar*) calendar to tell the date on a day-to-day basis, most traditional holidays are based on the old 음력 **umnyok** (*lunar*) calendar. Two of the most important festivals are 설날 **sollal** (*first day of the first lunar month*) and 추석 **chuseok** (*fifteenth day of the eighth lunar month*).

The climate

Korea has four distinct 계절 **kyejol** (*seasons*). 봄 **pom** (*spring*) from March to May is when the flowers bloom. Though the weather is mostly clear, there is a short period when sandy dust from China covers the country and reduces air quality. 여름 **yorum** (*summer*) from June to August is very hot and humid, particularly during the 장마 **jangma** (*monsoon*) season in July. 가을 **kaul** (*autumn*) is cool with wind and clear skies. Finally, 겨울 **kyoul** (*winter*) is cold and snowy with temperatures frequently falling below 0°C.

Find the festivals mentioned in the text. What Western holidays are most similar?

Vocabulary builder

03.01 Read the vocabulary and try to pronounce each word. Then listen and try to imitate the speakers.

DAYS OF THE WEEK

월요일	woryoil	*Monday*
화요일	hwayoil	*Tuesday*
수요일	suyoil	*Wednesday*
목요일	mogyoil	*Thursday*
금요일	kumyoil	*Friday*
토요일	thoyoil	*Saturday*
일요일	iryoil	*Sunday*

MONTHS OF THE YEAR

일월	ilwol	*January*	칠월	chilwol	*July*
이월	iwol	*February*	팔월	phalwol	*August*
삼월	samwol	*March*	구월	kuwol	*September*
사월	sawol	*April*	시월	siwol	*October*
오월	owol	*May*	십일월	sibilwol	*November*
유월	yuwol	*June*	십이월	sibiwol	*December*

NEW EXPRESSIONS

생일이 언제예요?	Saengiri onjeyeyo?	*When is your birthday?*
몇년생이에요?	Myonnyonsaengieyo?	*Which year were you born?*
무슨 요일이에요?	Musun yoil ieyo?	*What day is it?*
몇월 며칠이에요?	Myodwol myochil ieyo?	*What is the date?*
-년 -월 -일	-nyon -wol -il	*(yyyy/mm/dd) date order*
몇 시예요?	Myossi yeyo?	*What time is it?*
-시 -분	-si -pun	*(hh/mm) time order*
오전 / 오후	ojon/ohu	*a.m./p.m.*
오늘	onul	*today*
날씨가 어때요?	Nalssi ga ottaeyo?	*What is the weather like?*
좋아요 / 나빠요	Joayo/Nappayo.	*It is good/bad.*
따뜻해요 / 시원해요	Ttattuthaeyo/Chuwoyo.	*It is warm/cool.*
맑아요 / 흐려요	Malgayo/Hulyoyo.	*It is clear/cloudy.*

 Conversations

03.02 *Sangsu is asking Juri about the date, time and weather where she is. Listen and answer the questions.*

1 Is it the weekend?

상수	오늘 몇월 며칠이에요?
주리	팔월 이십이일이에요.
상수	무슨 요일이에요?
주리	화요일이에요.
상수	지금 몇 시예요?
주리	오후 두시 삼십사분이에요.
상수	오늘 날씨가 어때요?
주리	날씨가 좋아요! 따뜻해요. 그리고 맑아요.

2 Read or listen to the conversation again and answer these questions.
   a What is the date today?
   b What day of the week is it?
   c What is the time right now?
   d How does Juri describe the weather? Is it raining where she is?

3 Find the expressions in the conversation that mean:
   a day (of the week)   **e** weather
   b What day is it?   **f** What is the weather like?
   c afternoon   **g** and
   d What time is it?   **h** It is clear.

 4 <u>03.03</u> Answer Sangsu's questions yourself to state the date and time, and describe the weather where you are. Use the English prompts to help you.

Sangsu and Juri are finding out how old each other are. Listen and answer the questions.

5 Who is older: Sangsu or Juri?

상수	주리씨는 생일이 언제예요?
주리	제 생일은 사월 오일이에요.
상수	몇년생이에요?
주리	천구백구십일년생이에요. 상수씨는 생일이 언제예요?
상수	제 생일은 이월 이십일일이에요. 그리고 저는 천구백팔십칠년생이에요.
주리	그럼 상수씨는 몇 살이에요?
상수	저는 스물여섯살이에요. 주리씨는 몇 살이에요?
주리	저는 스물두살이에요.

6 Read or listen to the conversation again and answer these questions.

  a When is Juri's birthday? What year was Juri born?
  b When is Sangsu's birthday? What year was Sangsu born?
  c How old is Sangsu?
  d How old is Juri? Who is older?

7 Can you say the following in Korean?

  a My birthday is 30th September.
  b I was born in 1990.
  c I am 29 years old.

8 Read the following answers. What are the questions?

  a 목요일이에요.
  b 지금 오전 열한시 반이에요.
  c 오늘 11월 11일이에요.
  d 제 생일은 팔월 이십이일이에요.
  e 저는 천구백팔십일년생이에요.
  f 저는 서른한살이에요.

Language discovery

 Look at the phrases below and find the particles -이 and -가 that follow the nouns. Can you guess what these particles represent?

   a 생일이 언제예요? **Saengili onjeyeyo?**

   b 날씨가 좋아요. 날씨가 나빠요. **Nalssiga joayo. Nalssiga nappayo.**

1 THE SUBJECT PARTICLE: -이/가 -I/GA

In Korean, the subject particle -이/가 **-i/ga** marks the subject of a sentence – the person, place or thing that is <u>doing</u> something. For example, in the sentence *The man kicked the ball*, the *man* is the subject of the verb *kicked* and thus the subject of the sentence.

▶ The subject particle -이 attaches to nouns ending in a consonant.

▶ The subject particle -가 attaches to nouns ending in a vowel.

You will often find that the subject of a given sentence can also be the topic, in which case you'd be inclined to use the topic particle -은/는 **-un/nun**. This may cause confusion as to which particle to use. Don't worry too much as most sentences will be correct with both. Some sound more natural with one than the other, but you will gradually pick this up over time with practice. On the other hand, do not leave out particles as this confuses native speakers, even though they often leave them out themselves in casual speech!

2 ADJECTIVES = DESCRIPTIVE VERBS

In Korean, adjectives are presented in a similar fashion to verbs with -다 attached to the verb stem to create the dictionary form. Therefore, we call them descriptive verbs. The new weather-related phrases are descriptive verbs and their polite -요 forms have been derived using the same rules outlined for verbs in general.

3 SINO-KOREAN NUMBERS AS COUNTERS

When stating the date, you use Sino-Korean numbers as has been demonstrated. With telling the time it is slightly different. Pure Korean numbers are used for the hour, while Sino-Korean numbers are used for the minutes. Unlike pure Korean, Sino-Korean numbers are never altered when used as counters.

4 TIPS ON NUMBERS

Asking a person his/her age

Upon meeting, Koreans often ask each other 몇년생이에요? **Myonnyon saeng ieyo?** (*Which year were you born?*). The question is to establish each other's age and determine who is older. Confucian traditions highlight the importance of respect to elders and this way people are able to show the appropriate level of courtesy.

Saying the date and time

In Korean, dates and times are written in the order of the larger to the smaller units. For example, *22 minutes past 4 in the afternoon on 17th May 2012* would be written as 2012년 5월 17일 오후 4시 22분.

Months of the year

The months are the Sino-Korean numbers 1 to 12 combined with 월 **wol**, the word for *month* in Korean. Note, however, that *June* and *October* are slight exceptions since the numbers 6 and 10 lose their last letter to give 유월 and 시월 instead of 육월 and 십월.

Days of the week

Each day of the week represents one of the seven elements of the universe. Monday through Sunday, in respective order, represent the Moon, Fire, Water, Tree, Metal, Earth and Sun.

5 MORE WAYS TO DESCRIBE TIME AND WEATHER

-시 반	**-si pan**	*half past . . . (hour)*
-시 -분 전	**-si -pun jon**	*-minutes to . . . (hour)*
저녁	**jonyok**	*evening*
더워요 / 추워요	**Towoyo/Chuwoyo.**	*It is hot/cold.*
비가 와요	**Piga wayo.**	*It is raining.*
눈이 와요	**Nuni wayo.**	*It is snowing.*
바람이 불어요	**Parami puroyo.**	*It is windy.*

Practice

1 **Give the times and dates below in using the appropriate number system. Follow the example.**

Example: 6.32 p.m.   오후 여섯시 삼십이분

              2nd July 2012   이천십이년 칠월 이일

   a 10.09 a.m.   **e** 15th October 2001
   b 29/04/1982   **f** 5.55 p.m.
   c Quarter to 11 in the evening   **g** Thursday 31st December
   d 7.25 p.m.   **h** Sunday 16th June

2 **Complete the sentences with the correct subject particle.**

   a 오늘 날씨   ...(이/가)...   좋아요.
   b 저는 생일   ...(이/가)...   오월 일일이에요.
   c 지금 비   ...(이/가)...   와요.
   d 주리씨는 생일   ...(이/가)...   언제예요?
   e 오늘 눈   ...(이/가)...   와요.
   f 바람   ...(이/가)...   불어요.
   g 오늘 날짜   ...(이/가)...   몇월 며칠이에요?

3 <u>03.05</u> **Say your answers to the following questions out loud then listen and check your answers.**

   a Ask when Martin's birthday is. Then ask him how old he is. What will he answer if his birthday is 12th June and he is 31 years old?
   b Ask Sarah what year she was born. What will she say if she was born in 1976?
   c Ask what day of the week it is today.
   d Ask what the time is right now.
   e Say the weather is bad today. Say that it is windy and cold.
   f Say it is clear today. Also say it is hot.

Speaking

Sujin and Maria are talking about birthdays. Complete the conversation as Maria. Use the English prompts to help you.

Sujin	마리아씨 생일이 언제예요?
Maria	*Say your birthday is 25th October. Then ask when Sujin's birthday is.*
Sujin	제 생일은 시월 이일이에요. 마리아는 몇년생이에요?
Maria	*Say you were born in 1989.*
Sujin	우리 동생 수민이도 팔십구년생이에요.
Maria	*Ask when Sumin's birthday is.*
Sujin	팔월 삼십일이에요.
Maria	*Ask what year Sujin was born.*
Sujin	저는 천구백팔십칠년생이에요.

Listening

1 <u>03.06</u> **Listen and complete the dates and times in Korean. Then give the English for each.**

a _____ 오전 _____ 시   _____

b 십이월 _____ 일 오후 세시 _____   _____

c _____ 월 _____ 일 목요일 _____ 시 _____ 분   _____

d _____ 년 십일월 _____ 일   _____

e _____ 저녁 _____ 시 _____   _____

f 이천팔년 _____ 월 _____ 일 _____ 시 십칠분   _____

g 일월 _____ 일 _____ 한시 _____ 분   _____

h _____ 년 _____ 월 _____ 일   _____

2 <u>03.07</u> **Listen to the students talk about the weather in their areas today. Match the names and the pictures of the weather.**

a Junsu   **b** Minji   **c** Jihoon

1   **2**    **3**

Reading and writing

1 Read the passage written by Sumin then fill in the missing details.

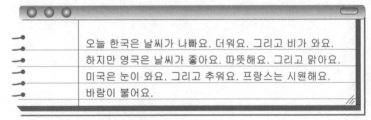

제 생일은 시월 십칠일이에요. 저는 스무살이에요.
사라는 열여덟살이에요. 사라 생일은 오월
이십팔일이에요. 지훈이는 스물한살이에요.
생일은 이월 구일이에요. 민지 생일은 십일월삼십일이
에요. 민지는 스물네살이에요.

Name	Age	Birthday
Sumin	a _____	b _____
Sarah	c _____	d _____
Jihun	e _____	f _____
Minji	g _____	h _____

2 Write a passage similar to Sumin's. Describe the ages and birthdays of your friends.

3 Read the passage and answer the following questions.

오늘 한국은 날씨가 나빠요. 더워요. 그리고 비가 와요.
하지만 영국은 날씨가 좋아요. 따뜻해요. 그리고 맑아요.
미국은 눈이 와요. 그리고 추워요. 프랑스는 시원해요.
바람이 불어요.

a What is the weather like today in Korea?
b Is it raining in England?
c In which country is it snowing?
d What is the weather like in France?

4 Keep a weather journal for the next few days. Write the date out in full each day to practise writing numbers in Korean.

Example:

Day 1   날짜: 이천십이년 사월 칠일 토요일
　　　　날씨: 오늘은 흐려요. 비가 와요.

Test yourself

1 How would you do the following?

   a State your date of birth.

   _____

   b Say the time.

   _____

   c Ask what the weather is like.

   _____

   d Give the numbers using pure Korean, then give them using Sino-Korean.

   69 _____   24 _____   45 _____   81 _____

2 Read the sentences. Find mistakes with the use of the subject particle and correct the errors.

   a 동생 생일가 언제예요?

   b 날씨가 좋아요.

   c 바람이 불어요.

   d 오늘 날짜이 어떻게 돼요?

3 Which number system would you use for each of following counters?

   a years of age   **d** hours (time)

   b minutes (time)   **e** day (date)

   c year (date)   **f** month (date)

SELF CHECK

	I CAN. . .
◯	. . . say how old I am and when my birthday is.
◯	. . . ask someone when his/her birthday is.
◯	. . . say what day it is.
◯	. . . tell someone the time.
◯	. . . describe the weather.

1 **Look at these names of countries in Korean. You should be able to recognize them. Read the names out loud then give the English equivalent.**

a 파키스탄 _____ f 덴마크 _____

b 멕시코 _____ g 인도네시아 _____

c 뉴질랜드 _____ h 폴란드 _____

d 네덜란드 _____ i 캐나다 _____

e 스웨덴 _____ j 싱가포르 _____

2 **Complete the sentences with the correct verb ending of the copula –이다. Is an honorific ending needed? Think carefully!**

a 저는 한국
  사람 _____.

b 우리 동생은
  변호사 _____.

c 우리 아버지는
  회사원 _____.

d 우리 어머니는
  요리사 _____.

e 우리 아내는
  미국사람 _____.

f 저는 학생 _____.

g 우리 할머니는
  여든여섯살 _____.

h 딸 이름은 안나 _____.

3 **Put the numbers in full in Korean. Note the counters in parentheses and choose the appropriate number system.**

a _____ 7 명 (people)

b _____ 38 살 (years of age)

c _____ 55 분 (minutes, time)

d _____ 2013 년 (year, date)

e _____ 3 시 (hours, time)

f _____ 6 월 (month, date)

g _____ 21 일 (day, date)

h _____ 1996 (year, date)

4 Eden and Thomas are penpals and have met for the first time online. Read their online chat conversation then answer the questions that follow.

이든	안녕하세요! 반가워요! 저는 이든이에요.
토마스	안녕하세요! 저는 토마스예요.
이든	토마스씨는 몇살이에요?
토마스	저는 스무살이에요. 이든씨는 몇살이에요?
이든	저도 스무살이에요! 천구백구십사년생이에요!
토마스	구십사년생! 오! 반가워요! 생일이 언제예요?
이든	십이월 십칠일이에요.
토마스	우리 여동생도 생일이 십이월이에요. 제 여동생 제나는 열다섯살이에요. 그리고 학생이에요.
이든	토마스씨는 가족이 몇 명이에요?
토마스	우리 가족은 모두 다섯 명이에요. 우리 부모님, 저, 우리 누나하고 여동생. 이든씨는 몇 명이에요?
이든	우리 가족은 모두 네 명이에요. 아버지, 어머니, 저하고 언니예요. 우리 언니는 회사원이에요. 그리고 나이는 스물네살이에요. 토마스씨 아버지는 성함이 어떻게 되세요?
토마스	우리 아버지는 빌 제라드세요. 미국 분이세요. 그리고 공무원이세요.
이든	우리 아버지는 선생님이세요.
토마스	이든씨, 지금 영국 날씨가 어때요? 좋아요?
이든	아니요 날씨가 나빠요. 비가 와요. 한국은 날씨가 어때요?
토마스	한국은 따뜻해요!

a How old is Eden? When is her exact date of birth?

b How old is Thomas? What year was he born?

c Which sentence means 'My younger sister's birthday is also in December'?

d How many people are in Thomas's family? Who are they? What relation is Jenna to Thomas?

e How many people are there in Eden's family? What does Eden's sister do for a living? Is she older or younger than Eden?

f Thomas's father is called Tim Gerrard. True or False?

g What nationality is Thomas's father? What is his occupation?

h What is the weather in England?

i Which country is Thomas in? What's the weather there?

물건 사기! 얼마예요?
Shopping! How much is it?

In this unit, you will learn how to:
▶ *ask for things in shops.*
▶ *ask the price.*
▶ *state quantities.*

CEFR: *(A1) Can understand and use simple sentences asking for items in a shop. (A1) Can handle numbers to state prices and quantities.*

🎥 Traditional markets

전통 시장 **jont^hong shijang** (*traditional markets*) are one of the most visited 관광지 **kwangwangji** (*tourist attractions*) in Korea. There are about 1,500 전통시장 in the country, eight of which are designated culture and tourism markets. The two biggest and most popular in Seoul are Dongdaemun Market, the centre of Korea's wholesale and retail fashion industries, and Namdaemun Market, a well-established market boasting 600 years of history and over 1,700 products.

As with any market, customers can try haggling prices to grab a bargain. If the 가격 **kagyok** (*price*) the seller calls is too high, you may say 너무 비싸요. 좀 깎아 주세요! **Nomu pissayo. Jom kkakka juseyo!** (*It's too expensive. Please give me a discount!*) Remember to stay polite. Greet the seller with안녕하세요 **annyonghaseyo** (*hello*), using the polite speech ending -요 **-yo**, and when leaving, say 안녕히 계세요 **annyonghi kyeseyo** (*goodbye*), and 많이 파세요! **Mani paseyo!** which means *Sell lots!*

As a 관광객 **kwangwanggaek** (*tourist*) you may find some stall owners and shop assistants over friendly or too hospitable. Customer satisfaction is hugely important in Korea with the belief that 손님이 왕이다 **sonnimi wangida** (*the customer is the king*).

💡 What can you say if a price is too high?
a 너무 비싸요.   **b** 안녕하세요   **c** 관광지

Vocabulary builder

<u>04.01</u> **Read the vocabulary and try to pronounce each word. Then listen and try to imitate the speakers.**

AT A SMALL SHOP

빵	ppang	*bread*
우유	uyu	*milk*
과자	kwaja	*biscuits*
주스	jusu	*juice*
라면	ramyon	*ramen*
물	mul	*water*
책	chaek	*book*
사과	sagwa	*apple*
영수증	yongsujung	*receipt*

NEW EXPRESSIONS

어서오세요.	Oso oseyo.	*Welcome.*
뭘 찾으세요?	Mwol chajuseyo?	*What are you looking for?*
. . . 있어요?	. . . issoyo?	*Do you have . . . ?*
. . . 주세요	. . . juseyo.	*Please give me . . .*
-에 . . . 원이에요.	-e . . . won ieyo.	*It is . . . won per - items.*
(모두) 얼마예요?	(modu) Olmayeyo?	*How much is it (altogether)?*
고맙습니다.	Komapsumnida.	*Thank you.*
안녕히 가세요.	Annyonghi kaseyo.	*Goodbye (to person leaving).*
안녕히 계세요.	Annyonghi kyeseyo.	*Goodbye (to person staying).*
. . . 가지	. . . kaji	*. . . (different) kinds*
-개	-kae	*-items (basic counting unit)*
-권	-kwon	*-books (counter)*
-병	-byong	*-bottles (counter)*

> **COUNTERS (COUNTING WORDS)**
> Counters are used to count objects. For example, in *two* <u>bottles</u> *of coke,* <u>bottles</u> is a counter. Age (years), hours and minutes are also counters. Each counter uses a different number system. When counting items, pure Korean numbers are used.

 Conversations

04.02 *Yerin is looking for a particular item. Janghun works at the shop and offers to help. Listen and answer the questions.*

1 What is Yerin shopping for?

장훈	안녕하세요. 어서오세요.
예린	안녕하세요. 주스 있어요?
장훈	네. 주스 두 가지 있어요. 사과 주스와 오렌지 주스 있어요.
예린	사과 주스는 얼마예요?
장훈	한 병에 팔백원이에요.
예린	그럼 오렌지 주스는 얼마예요?
장훈	한 병에 칠백오십원이에요.
예린	사과 주스 한 병하고 오렌지 주스 한 병 주세요. 모두 얼마예요?
장훈	모두 천오백오십원이에요.
예린	영수증도 주세요.
장훈	여기 있어요. 고맙습니다. 안녕히 가세요.
예린	고맙습니다. 안녕히 계세요.

2 Read or listen to the conversation again and answer these questions.

   a How many kinds of the item does Janghun have? How much are they each?

   b How many items does Yerin buy?

   c How much is the total?

   d What does Yerin also ask for?

3 Can you say the following in Korean?

   a I have five kinds of ramen.

   b I have Samdasu water and Volvic water.

   c It is 1,200 won per bottle.

   d It is 3,700 won in total.

 4 04.03 **Imagine you are the shop assistant. Help Yerin with her shopping. What does she want to buy this time? Use the English prompts to help you.**

Yerin returns the next day to buy some more items. This time Duho is working at the shop. Listen and answer the questions.

5 How many different items does Yerin buy in total?

두호	어서오세요. 뭘 찾으세요?
예린	안녕하세요. 우유 있어요?
두호	네. 우유 있어요. 세 가지 있어요. 일반 우유와 초코 우유하고 딸기 우유 있어요.
예린	일반 우유는 얼마예요? 그리고 초코 우유하고 딸기 우유는 얼마예요?
두호	일반 우유는 한 개에 삼백원, 초코 우유는 오백원, 그리고 딸기 우유는 한 개에 사백원이에요.
예린	일반 우유 한 개 주세요. 그리고 사과하고 과자 주세요. 책도 한 권 주세요. 그럼 모두 얼마예요?
두호	모두 이만팔천육백원이에요.
예린	여기 있어요. 고맙습니다. 안녕히 계세요.
두호	고맙습니다. 안녕히 가세요.

6 Read or listen to the conversation again and answer these questions.

  a How many different kinds of milk does the shop sell?

  b What is the price difference between the most expensive and cheapest milk?

  c Does Yerin buy coffee and tissues too?

  d How much is it altogether?

7 Find the underlined words in the conversation then cover the conversation up. Can you say them in Korean?

  a Do you have <u>milk</u>?

  b I have <u>plain</u> milk, <u>chocolate</u>-flavoured milk and <u>strawberry</u>-flavoured milk.

  c <u>How much</u> is the plain milk?

  d The strawberry-flavoured milk is <u>400 won per carton</u>.

  e <u>Please give me</u> one carton of plain milk.

  f Please give me <u>one book</u> too.

  g Here it is/<u>Here you are</u>.

  h <u>Thank you</u>. Goodbye (to person staying).

Language discovery

 Find these sentences in the last conversation. Which particles are used after nouns to list numerous items?

   a Please give me one bottle of apple juice and one bottle of orange juice.
   b I have plain milk, chocolate-flavoured milk and strawberry-flavoured milk.
   c Please give me one carton of plain milk. Also please give me apples and biscuits. Please give me a book too.

1 PARTICLES FOR 'AND': -하고 -*HAGO*, -와/과 -*WA/GWA*

-하고 **-hago** and -와/과 **-wa/gwa** are used between two nouns to connect them with *and*. -하고, in general, is used in informal situations, and -와/과 is used in writing and in formal situations.

▶ -하고 **-hago** is used for all nouns regardless of the noun's spelling.
▶ -와/과 **-wa/gwa** are used separately depending on the last letter of the preceding noun.
   ▷ -와 *is used after nouns ending in a vowel, as in* 사과와 물 **sakwawa mul**.
   ▷ -과 *is used after nouns ending in a consonant, as in* 물과 사과 **mulgwa sakwa**.

2 PARTICLE FOR 'ALSO': -도 -*DO*

-도 **-do** is translated as *also* or *too* and comes after a noun, regardless of how it is spelled. The sentence 책 한 권도 주세요 **chaek han kwondo juseyo** translates into *Please give me a book too* or *Please also give me a book*.

3 SENTENCE ORDER FOR COUNTERS

When a counting unit is combined with the name of an object in a sentence, the object comes first, followed by the number and the counting unit. For example, *Please give me one (unit of) bread* becomes 빵 한 개 주세요 **ppang han gae juseyo**. The object 빵 is followed by the number 한, then the counting unit 개 and finally the verb as all Korean sentences end with the verb.

4 STATING PRICES: (-에) . . . 원이에요 *(-E) . . . IEYO*

. . . 원이에요 **. . . won ieyo** states how much an item is. If you want to specify the price of an item per a certain quantity you can use the particle -에 **-e** after the specific quantity as in the following examples:

책 한 권에 만원이에요.	**Chaek han kwon e manwon ieyo.**	*It is 10,000 won per book.*
주스 한 병에 사백원이에요.	**Jusu han byong e sabaegwon ieyo.**	*It is 400 won per bottle of juice.*
사과 세 개에 삼백원이에요.	**Sagwa se gae e sambaegwon ieyo.**	*It is 300 won per three apples.*

5 POLITE REQUESTS: -(으)세요 *-(U)SEYO*

-(으)세요 **-(u)seyo** is used after a verb stem to make a command or request. It is used in informal situations to social superiors and elders, as well as to peers you are not particularly close to or have met for the first time. In this unit this verb ending is used between the shop assistant and customer who are not acquainted.

▶ If the verb stem ends in a vowel, -세요 **-seyo** is used.

The main request introduced in the conversations is 주세요 **juseyo** meaning *Please give me . . . .* The verb *to give* 주다 **juda** has the stem 주- **ju-**. Since this ends in a vowel **u**, the ending -세요 is used to create the request 주세요.

▶ If the verb stem ends in a consonant, -으세요 is used.

For example the verb *to sit* 앉다 **antta** has the stem 앉- **anj-**. With the -으세요 ending you get the request (*Please sit*) 앉으세요 **anjuseyo**.

You will notice the phrase 뭘 찾으세요? **Mwol chajuseyo?** also has a similar ending but isn't a command or request. This ending -으세요 combines an honorific (-(으)시-) with a polite ending (-어요). The verb *to look for* 찾다 **chatta** has the stem 찾- **chat-** ending in a consonant, and so uses the ending -으세요 to form the question 찾으세요? **Chajuseyo?**, with the ending used to show respect for the subject of the sentence (here, a customer).

Practice

1 Choose the correct particle or word to connect and complete the sentences. Which *and* or *also* is needed to complete the lists? Go back to the lesson for help.

a 빵	. . . (와/과) . . .	우유 주세요.
b 사과 한 개	. . . (와/과) . . .	쥬스 한 병 주세요.
c 라면	. . . (와/과) . . .	우유 있어요?
d 우유	. . . (과/하고) . . .	빵 주세요.
e 휴지	. . . (과/하고) . . .	비누 있어요?
f 배	. . . (와/하고) . . .	사과는 얼마예요?
g 물	. . . (와/하고) . . .	쥬스는 얼마예요?
h 커피	. . . (하고/그리고) . . .	우유 주세요.
i 물 있어요?	. . . (하고/그리고) . . .	라면은 얼마예요?
j 영수증	. . . (그리고/도) . . .	주세요.
k 사과 있어요.	. . . (그리고/도) . . .	배는 한 개에 오백원이에요.
l 계란하고 커피	. . . (그리고/도) . . .	주세요. 모두 얼마예요?

2 <u>04.05</u> **Say the following out loud then listen and check your answers.**

a Say you have four kinds of water. Then say you also have seven kinds of juice.

b Say it is 38,100 won in total.

c Ask for a receipt. Then say 'thank you'.

d Ask for ten books, bread, a carton of milk and two bottles of juice.

e Say 'welcome' and then ask the customer what they are looking for. What will the customer say if they want to buy three packets of ramen?

f Ask if the shop has apples. Ask how much they are. What will the shop assistant answer if they are 5,000 won per three apples?

Speaking

You are shopping. Janghun, the shop assistant, offers to help. Complete the conversation . Use the English prompts to help you.

Janghun	안녕하세요. 뭘 찾으세요?
You	*Ask if they have bread.*
Janghun	네. 빵 두 가지 있어요. 팥빵하고 크림빵 있어요.
You	*Ask how much the cream-filled bread* (크림빵) *is.*
Janghun	크림빵은 팔백원이에요. 그리고 세 개에 이천원이에요.
You	*Ask for three cream-filled breads. Also ask if they sell milk.*
Janghun	우유 없어요. 주스는 있어요. 사과 주스하고 오렌지 주스 있어요.
You	*Ask for a bottle of apple juice and a bottle of orange juice.*
Janghun	여기 있어요.
You	*Ask how much it is altogether. Also ask for a receipt.*
Janghun	모두 오천구백팔십원이에요.
You	*Say 'Here you go'. Then say 'thank you' and 'goodbye'.*
Janghun	고맙습니다. 안녕히 가세요.

Listening

1 <u>04.06</u> **Listen to the conversation and answer the questions.**

  a What item does Yerin ask for first? How many does she buy?
  b What else does she ask for? Does she ask for any biscuits?
  c What is the difference in price of the two ramen Janghun has to offer?
  d How many bottles of water does she buy?
  e How much is her shopping altogether? Does she ask for a receipt?

2 <u>04.07</u> **Listen to the prices. Fill in the missing numbers.**

  a 7 _ _ 원   **e** 1 2 _ 0 _ _ 원
  b _ 6 _ _ 원   **f** _ _ 9 2 0 원
  c 5 _ _ 0 0 원   **g** _ _ _ 0 원
  d _ _ 8 _ 4 원   **h** _ _ 3 7 _ _ 원

Reading and writing

1 Look at Yerin's receipt. Then read the statements and answer true, false or uncertain.

과자	2	3,800
책	1	9,900
빵	1	1,100
사과	4	6,000
라면	3	2,100
주스	2	1,700
Total		229,000

a Yerin bought milk and pears.

b The bread was 1,100 won.

c Yerin bought apple juice.

d The book cost less than 10,000 won.

e The shop didn't have any water.

f 사과는 한 개에 이천원이에요.

g 라면 한 개에 칠백원이에요.

h 빵하고 책 있어요.

i 모두 이십구만이천원이에요.

2 Mina sends her non-Korean speaking friend Susie to the shops with the following note. What items should Susie bring back with her?

> 안녕하세요! 주스 두 병과 빵 한 개와 라면 한 개 주세요.
> 사과 다섯 개와 책 세 권도 주세요. 그리고 영수증도
> 주세요. 고맙습니다! 안녕히 계세요.

1 _____   **4** _____

2 _____   **5** _____

3 _____   **6** _____

3 Mina needs more items from the shop. Write a memo similar to the one in the previous question for Susie to take with her. Include two bottles of water, three ramen, one carton of milk, four packets of biscuits, six apples and a receipt. Use the glossary to find vocabulary items if needed.

Test yourself

1 How would you do the following?

a Ask the price of apples. Ask the price per three apples. Then ask how much it is in total.

_____

b Ask for three packets of biscuits, a bottle of water and a receipt.

_____

c Say 'goodbye' to the shop assistant who is staying. Say 'goodbye' to a customer who is leaving.

_____

d Give the numbers in parentheses in full, using the appropriate number system. Note the counters.

1 (3)_____ 개   **3** (10) _____ 권   **5** (9,050) _____ 원

2 (1) _____ 병   **4** (4) _____ 가지   **6** (20,000) _____ 원

2 What do these particles mean in Korean?

a -과   **c** -하고

b -도   **d** -와

3 Complete the sentences with an appropriate counter for each item.

a 사과 다섯 _____ 에 이천원.   **d** 주스 한 _____ 은 얼마예요?

b 물 한 _____ 주세요.   **e** 책 세 _____ 에 오만원.

c 과자 한 _____ 주세요.   **f** 모두 만팔천구백 _____
                                   이에요.

SELF CHECK

I CAN. . .

- ○ . . . ask for one item or a list of items with *have/give*.
- ○ . . . state the quantity of items needed.
- ○ . . . ask the price of items and the final shopping total.
- ○ . . . state and list the kinds of items in a shop.

5

음식 주문하기!
뭐 먹을래요?

Ordering food!
What do you want to eat?

In this unit, you will learn how to:
▶ *order food and drink.*
▶ *describe your meal.*
▶ *comment on your food.*

CEFR: *(A2) Can understand and use common expressions for ordering and dining in a restaurant. (A1) Can use basic phrases to describe and comment on a meal.*

Dining out

A Korean 식사 **siksa** (*meal*) usually consists of 밥 **pap** (*rice*), a 국 **kuk** (*soup*) or 찌개 **jjigae** (*stew*) and several 반찬 **panchan** (*side dishes*) including the very popular 김치 **kimchi**, a fermented cabbage dish with traditional seasonings. All dishes are set on the table at once and will come with a 숟가락 **sukkarak** (*spoon*) and 젓가락 **jokkarak** (*chopsticks*); most food is bite-sized so a knife is not needed.

In dining etiquette, it is polite to say 잘 먹겠습니다! **jal mokkessumnida!** before you eat to show you are looking forward to the meal, especially if you are at a person's home, and after, to say 잘 먹었습니다! **jal mogossumnida!**. Be sure to avoid making noises and, most important, don't blow your nose at the table. Ever. Last, there are many shared 반찬 so also avoid digging into bowls and touching food you are not taking.

You may call out 여기요! **yogiyo!** (*Over here please!*) in a 식당 **sikdang** (*restaurant*) to catch the waiter's attention. You will hardly ever need to ask for the 계산서 **kyesanso** (*bill*), which isn't typically given out. One pays at the front of the restaurant on the way out and does not leave a tip – there is no tipping system in ordinary restaurants.

 If 잘 먹겠습니다 before the meal means *I will eat well*, what would you expect 잘 먹었습니다 after the meal to mean?

Vocabulary builder

05.01 **Read the vocabulary and try to pronounce each word. Then listen and try to imitate the speakers.**

FOOD AND DRINK

음식, 음료수	umsik, umnyosu	*food, drinks*
녹차	nokcha	*green tea*
맥주	maekju	*beer*
갈비	kalbi	*beef/pork ribs*
삼겹살	samgyopsal	*pork belly*
불고기	bulgogi	*marinated beef BBQ*
비빔밥	bibimbap	*rice with seasoned vegetables*
김치찌개	kimchi jjigae	*kimchi stew*
된장찌개	twenjang jjigae	*soy bean paste stew*

NEW EXPRESSIONS

몇 분이세요?	Myoppuniseyo?	*How many of you are there?*
이 쪽으로 앉으세요.	I jjoguro anjuseyo.	*Please sit over here.*
뭐 먹을래요?	Mwo mogulleyo?	*What do you want to eat?*
… 먹을래요.	… mogullaeyo.	*I want to eat …*
… 먹을게요.	… mogulkkeyo	*I will eat …*
주문하시겠어요?	Jumun hasigessoyo?	*Would you like to order?*
맛있게 드세요.	Mashikke tuseyo.	*Enjoy your meal.*
음식이 어떠세요?	Umsigi ottoseyo?	*How is the food?*
맛있어요	Mashissoyo.	*It is tasty.*
조금	jogum	*slightly, a little*
정말 / 너무	jongmal/nomu	*very, really/too, exceedingly*
매워요.	Maewoyo.	*It is spicy.*
짜요 / 싱거워요	Jjayo/Shingowoyo	*It is salty./It is bland.*
죄송합니다.	Jwesonghamnida.	*I'm sorry.*
다시 해드릴까요?	Tashi hae turilkkayo?	*Shall we cook it again for you?*
다시 해주세요.	Tashi hae juseyo.	*Please cook it again for me.*
-잔 / -인분	-jan/-inbun	*-glasses, cups/-portions (counters)*

 Conversations

05.02 *Minjae and Taemin are in a restaurant. Suji, their waitress, is greeting them and is going to be serving them. Listen and answer the questions.*

1 For how many people does Minjae get a table?

수지	어서오세요. 몇 분이세요?
민재	두 명이에요.
수지	이 쪽으로 앉으세요.
민재	고맙습니다.
수지	음료수 주문하시겠어요?
태민	녹차 두 잔 주세요. 민재씨, 뭐 먹을래요?
민재	저는 비빔밥을 먹을래요.
태민	그럼 저는 된장찌개를 먹을게요.
수지	음식 주문하시겠어요?
태민	비빔밥 일 인분하고 된장찌개 일 인분 주세요.
수지	죄송합니다. 오늘 된장찌개가 없어요.
태민	그럼 비빔밥 이 인분 주세요.

2 Read or listen to the conversation again and answer these questions.
   a What drink does Taemin order? How many glasses does he order?
   b What does Minjae want to eat? What dish does Taemin choose?
   c What is the problem with Taemin's dish? What does he choose to eat instead?
   d What is the final food order?
   e Which number systems do the counters -잔 and -인분 use?

3 Can you say the following in Korean?
   a There are four of us.
   b I want to eat bibimbap. I will eat bibimbap.
   c Sorry. We don't have beer today.

 4 05.03 **Imagine you are at the restaurant with Minjae. Find out what he wants to eat so you can order lunch. Use the English prompts to help you.**

Minjae and Taemin return to the restaurant later in the day for dinner, but there is a problem with their meal. Listen to their conversation and answer the questions.

수지	음료수 주문하시겠어요?
민재	네. 맥주 두 병하고 콜라 한 병 주세요.
태민	음식도 지금 주문할게요. 삼겹살 있어요?
수지	네. 삼겹살 있어요.
태민	그럼 삼겹살 이 인분 주세요. 그리고 김치 찌개 일 인분 주세요.

A while later, Suji brings the order . . .

수지	여기 있어요. 맛있게 드세요.
민재	고맙습니다. 잘 먹겠습니다.

After trying the food Taemin calls Suji . . .

태민	여기요!
수지	네. 음식이 어떠세요?
태민	삼겹살이 너무 짜요. 그리고 김치 찌개가 조금 매워요.
수지	죄송합니다. 다시 해드릴까요?
태민	네. 다시 해주세요.

5 **Read or listen to the conversation again and answer these questions.**
   a What is the final drinks and food order?
   b What is the problem with the food?
   c What does Suji offer to do?

6 **Say the sentences in Korean.**
   a I'll order food now as well, please.
   b Do you have pork belly?
   c Here you go. Enjoy your meal.

7 **Can you translate the following into English?**
   a 고맙습니다. 잘 먹겠습니다.
   b 여기요!
   c 죄송합니다. 다시 해드릴까요?

Language discovery

Find these expressions in the last conversation. Translate them into English and notice the different verb endings.

a 뭐 먹을래요? 저는 비빔밥을 먹을래요. 저는 비빔밥을 먹을게요.

b 주문하시겠어요?

c 다시 해드릴까요? 다시 해주세요.

1 THE OBJECT PARTICLE: -을/를 *-UL/-LUL*

A direct object in a sentence is the person, place, or thing that receives the action of a verb (or shows the result of the action). For example, in *he drinks beer* and *I eat kalbi*, *beer* and *kalbi* are the objects of the actions drink and eat (drinks what? beer; eats what? kalbi). Korean marks objects by adding the object particle -을/를 **-ul/lul** to the noun which is the object of the sentence.

▶ -를 is used after a vowel; -을 after a consonant.

Note, however, that the verbs 있어요 **issoyo** and 없어요 **opssoyo** <u>never take objects</u>. This means you will see sentences in the form of 책이 있어요 **chaegi issoyo** (*I have books*), but never see a sentence like 책을 있어요 **chaegul issoyo**.

2 TO WANT TO DO SOMETHING: -(으)ㄹ래요 *-(U)LLAEYO*

-(으)ㄹ래요 **-(u)llaeyo** is attached to a verb stem to express a desire, preference or intention. Used in the first or second person, this ending generally translates as *want* (to do something).

▶ If the verb stem ends in a vowel or ㄹ, -ㄹ래요 is used.
▶ If the verb stem ends in a consonant other than ㄹ, -을래요 is used.

To illustrate, stems 팔- **pʰal-** and 마시- **mashi-** use -ㄹ래요 to give 팔래요 **pʰallaeyo** (*I want to sell*) and 마실래요 **mashillaeyo** (*I want to drink*). The stem 먹- **mok-** uses -을래요 to give 먹을래요 **mogullaeyo** (*I want to eat*).

Study these examples from previous conversations: 저는 비빔밥을 먹을래요 **Jonun pibimbabul mogullaeyo** (*I <u>want</u> to eat bibimbap*); 뭐 먹을래요? **Mwo mogullaeyo?** (*What do you <u>want</u> to eat?*)

3 TO SAY YOU WILL DO SOMETHING: -(으)ㄹ게요 -(U)LKKEYO

The ending -(으)ㄹ게요 **-(u)lkkeyo** is used when the speaker is promising or volunteering to perform an action in the immediate future, or when s/he <u>will</u> do something. It is used almost entirely for the first person:

▶ ㄹ게요 is used for verb stems ending in a vowel such as 마시- **mashi-**, for example 마실게요 **mashilkkeyo** (*I will drink*).

▶ -을게요 is used for those ending in a consonant such as 먹- **mok-**, for example 먹을게요 **mogulkkeyo** (*I will eat*).

4 POLITE QUESTIONS: -(으)시겠어요? -(U)SIGESSOYO?

This verb ending is used to ask polite questions meaning *Would you like to…?*

▶ -시겠어요 **-sigessoyo** is used for verb stems ending in a vowel.

▶ -으시겠어요 **-usigessoyo** is used for verb stems ending in a consonant.

For example, the verb *to order* with stem 주문하- **jumunha-** uses -시겠어요 to become 주문하시겠어요? **jumunhasigessoyo**? (*Would you like to order?*) and the verb *to sit* with verb stem 앉- **anj-** uses -으시겠어요 to become 앉으시겠어요? **anjusigessoyo**? (*Would you like to sit?*)

5 SUGGESTIONS: -(으)ㄹ까요? -(U)LKKAYO?

-(으)ㄹ까요 **-(u)lkkayo** attached to a verb stem, when used in first person, makes a suggestion and translates as *Shall I . . . ?* or *Shall we . . . ?* For example, the question *Shall we cook it again for you?* becomes 다시 해 드릴까요? **tashi hae turilkkayo?**.

▶ -ㄹ까요 **-lkkayo** is attached after a vowel.

▶ -을까요 **-ulkkayo** is used after a consonant.

6 POLITE REQUESTS FOR MY BENEFIT: -(어/아) 주세요 -(O/A) JUSEYO

The verb 주다 **juda** as a main verb on its own means *to give*, but when used within the construction -(어/아) 주세요 **-(o/a) juseyo**, the speaker can make a request even more polite and stress that it is <u>for his/her own benefit</u>. For example, *Please do it for me (for my benefit)* would be 해 주세요 **hae juseyo**. The literal meaning is *please do it and give*, which, when put together, implies you are asking for it to be done for your benefit.

Practice

1 **Complete the sentences with the correct object particle. Which of the expressions should <u>not</u> use object particles? Why?**

   a 저는 비빔밥   …(을/를)…   먹을게요.
   b 김치 찌개   …(을/를)…   주문할게요.
   c 갈비   …(을/를)…   다시 해주세요.
   d 저는 맥주   …(을/를)…   마실게요.
   e 삼겹살   …(을/를)…   있어요?
   f 녹차   …(을/를)…   없어요.

2 **Read the sentences in English then complete them in Korean with the correct verb ending.**

   a I want to eat Kalbi.   갈비 먹   …(을래요/을게요).
   b I will eat Kalbi.   갈비 먹   …(을래요/을게요).
   c What do you want to eat?   뭐 먹   …(을래요/을게요)?
   d Shall we eat Kalbi?   갈비 먹   …(을까요/를까요)?
   e Would you like to eat Kalbi? 갈비 드시 …(어 주세요/겠어요)?
   f Please eat the Kalbi for me. 갈비 먹   …(어 주세요/겠어요).

3 <u>05.05</u> **Say the following out loud then listen and check your answers.**

   a Say you want to eat bibimbap. Then order a portion of bibimbap.
   b Say you will drink beer. Then order a glass of beer.
   c Ask a customer if they would like to order drinks. Then ask if they would like to order food too.
   d Ask the customer how their food is. What will the customer say if their dish is very tasty?
   e Say your kimchi stew is bland and too spicy. What will the waitress say if she offers to re-cook the dish for you?

Speaking

You are in a restaurant to order a take-away. Suji, the waitress, waits on you. Complete the conversation. Use the English prompts to help you.

Suji 어서 오세요. 주문하시겠어요?
You   *Ask if they have Bulgogi.*
Suji 죄송합니다. 불고기가 없어요. 갈비하고 삼겹살은 있어요.
You   *Ask for two portions of ribs and a bottle of water.*
Suji 네. 여기 있어요. 맛있게 드세요.

You return later to complain about your meal.

You   *Say your ribs are too salty.*
Suji   죄송합니다. 갈비 다시 해드릴까요?
You   *Say yes, please cook them again for me.*
Suji   갈비 이 인분 여기 있어요. 이번엔 음식이 어떠세요?
You   *Say it is very tasty. Thank the waitress and say goodbye.*
Suji   고맙습니다. 안녕히 가세요.

Listening

1 <u>05.06</u> **Listen to the conversation and answer the questions.**
   a How many people are there in the group? List their names.
   b What drinks do they order first?
   c What is the final food order?
   d Which additional drinks do they order with their meal? How many?

2 <u>05.07</u> **Listen to customers talk about their meals. Then read the statements and answer true, false, or uncertain.**
   a Minjae's kimchi stew is very tasty.
   b Jimin ordered ribs and bibimbap.
   c Taemin asked for his stew to be cooked again.
   d Jieun's marinated beef BBQ is slightly bland.
   e Janghun is very satisfied with his meal.

Reading and writing

1 **Read the bill and answer the questions.**
   a What was the most expensive dish ordered?
   b How many portions of pork belly were ordered?
   c Did the table order any portions of bibimbap?
   d How many soft drinks were ordered?
   e How many alcoholic drinks were ordered?
   f How much was the final bill? Write the number in Korean in full.

아리랑 식당		
2	김치 찌개	12,000
1	된장 찌개	8,000
3	삼겹살	21,000
1	맥주	4,000
2	녹차	3,000
		48,000

2 **Read the menu and answer true or false.**

   a Soy bean paste stew is
   4,000 won.

   b The most expensive
   dish is 10,000 won per
   portion.

   c This restaurant doesn't
   sell any alcoholic drinks.

   d 불고기는 일 인분에
   팔천원이에요.

   e 삼겹살 없어요.
   불고기하고 갈비만
   있어요.

   f 주스는 한 잔에
   삼천원이에요.

메뉴	
삼겹살	7,000
된장찌개	5,000
김치찌개	6,000
불고기	8,000
갈비 (2인분)	20,000
맥주	4,000
녹차	2,000
주스	3,000

3 **You are buying a takeaway lunch for**
yourself and a colleague. Sarah sends
you this text message. Send a reply
using the menu from the previous
question. Don't forget to ask Sarah
what she wants to eat.

된장찌개 있어요? 얼마예요?
저 삼겹살도 좋아해요. 삼겹살
있어요? 삼겹살은 얼마예요?
고마워요!

4 **This time Sarah goes to buy lunch. She**
sent you this text telling you what there
is to eat. Send her a reply with your
lunch order. Don't forget to ask her how
much the total is.

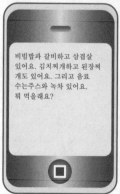

비빔밥과 갈비하고 삼겹살
있어요. 김치찌개하고 된장찌
개도 있어요. 그리고 음료
수는주스와 녹차 있어요.
뭐 먹을래요?

Test yourself

1 How would you do the following?

  a Ask how many there are in the group, seat them, and ask if they are ready to order.

  _____

  b Order three portions of ribs, one portion of kimchi stew, two portions of soy bean paste stew, two bottles of beer and one cup of green tea.

  _____

  c Say the food is very tasty. Thank the waitress and say you enjoyed the meal.

  _____

  d Say the pork belly is too salty and the bibimbap is slightly spicy. Then ask for the dishes to be cooked again.

  _____

2 Match the endings to the situations.

  a -(으)시겠어요?   **1** Make a polite request for my own benefit.
  b -(으)ㄹ게요   **2** Say you want to do something.
  c -(으)ㄹ까요?   **3** Say you will do something.
  d -(어/아) 주세요   **4** Make a suggestion.
  e -(으)ㄹ래요   **5** Make a polite question.

3 What would the preceding word's final letter be? Put V for vowel or C for consonant.

  a _____ -을래요   **e** _____ -을까요?
  b _____ -를   **f** _____ -을
  c _____ -시겠어요?   **g** _____ -으시겠어요?
  d _____ -을게요   **h** _____ -ㄹ게요

SELF CHECK

I CAN...
... ask a friend what s/he wants to eat.
... say what I'd like to eat.
... order food and drink.
... describe and comment on my food.

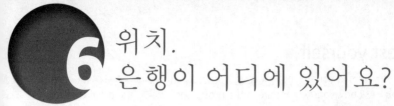

6 위치.
은행이 어디에 있어요?

Location. Where is the bank?

In this unit, you will learn how to:
▶ *ask for directions to find a destination.*
▶ *describe the location of a certain place.*
▶ *give directions to reach a destination.*

CEFR: *(A1) Can recognize and use basic phrases describing a location in relation to its surroundings. (A2) Can ask for and give directions to a point of interest using frequently used expressions.*

Finding your way

If you were to get a 택시 (*taxi*) and present the 운전기사 (*driver*) with the 주소 (*address*) of your 목적지 (*destination*), most drivers will use a satellite navigation system based on street names and numbers. However, if you were to ask 길 좀 알려주세요 (*please show me the way*) of a 행인 (*passer-by*), he will give you directions using nearby landmarks and 지하철 역 (*subway stations*), in particular, the specific 출구 번호 (*station exit number*). Moreover, many 명함 (*business cards*) and 전단지 (*leaflets*) have a 지도 (*map*) printed on the back depicting their exact 위치 (*location*) as this may be clearer than the address.

Why? In Korea, addresses used to be assigned chronologically by a building's construction date rather than geographically. Many streets had no names and were only recognized by their apartments or shops. A new improved system, similar to that of the West, has recently been introduced. Now, buildings are numbered consecutively and all streets are newly named. However, old habits die hard; the new system will take some time to get used to and many people still prefer to get and give directions in the old way.

If a passer-by told you to go to 1번 출구, where would you go?

a bus stop for the number 1 bus
b subway station exit number 1
c taxi stand

Vocabulary builder

06.01 **Read the vocabulary and try to pronounce each word. Then listen and try to imitate the speakers.**

POINTS OF INTEREST

학교	*school*
우체국	*post office*
백화점	*department store*
영화관	*cinema*
병원	*hospital*
은행	*bank*
슈퍼마켓	*supermarket*
미용실	*hair salon*
서점	*book store*
약국	*pharmacy*
신호등	*traffic lights*
횡단보도	*zebra crossing*
사거리	*crossroad*
… 역 -번 출구	*… station, exit no. -*

NEW EXPRESSIONS

실례합니다.	*Excuse me.*
어디에 있어요?	*Where is it?*
… 보이세요?	*Can you see … ?*
여기서 건너가세요.	*Cross here.*
… 미터 쯤 걸어가세요.	*Walk approximately … metres.*
(똑바로) 가세요	*Go … (straight ahead)*
왼쪽/오른쪽으로 가세요.	*Turn left/right.*
옆에, 사이에, 건너편에	*next to, in between, opposite*
앞에, 뒤에, 근처에	*in front, behind, near*
왼쪽에, 오른쪽에	*on the left, on the right*
이 쪽으로, 저 쪽으로	*in this direction, in that direction*
여기, 저기, 거기	*here, over there, there*

 Conversations

06.02 Taehee is asking a passer-by for directions to the local bank and supermarket. Listen and answer the questions.

1 Is there a department store nearby?

태희	실례합니다. 근처에 은행이 있어요?
행인	네, 있어요.
태희	어디에 있어요?
행인	저기 영화관 보이세요? 그 뒤에 백화점도 보이세요? 영화관과 백화점 사이에 있어요. 여기서 횡단보도를 건너가세요. 그리고 저 쪽으로 백 미터 쯤 걸어가시면 거기에 은행이 있어요.
태희	고맙습니다. 그리고 슈퍼마켓은 어디에 있어요?
행인	슈퍼마켓은 은행 건너편에 있어요. 하나 슈퍼마켓이에요. 약국 옆에 있어요.
태희	고맙습니다! 안녕히 가세요!

2 Read or listen to the conversation again and answer these questions.

   a Between which two buildings is the bank located?
   b Roughly how far away is the bank from where they are?
   c Where is the supermarket located in relation to the bank?
   d What is the supermarket called?

3 Can you say the following in Korean?

   a Is there a hospital nearby? Where is it?
   b It is between the book store and pharmacy.
   c If you walk about 200 metres in this direction there is a supermarket there.
   d It is next to the department store.
   e The school is located across from the cinema.

 4 *06.03 You are walking down the street and Taehee asks for directions to the book store. Help her find her way there. Use the English prompts to help you.*

Junki is on the phone to a customer who is trying to find his restaurant. Listen to Junki give directions and answer the questions.

5 What is the name of the restaurant the customer is looking for?

손님	아리랑 식당이 어디에 있어요?
준기	지금 뭐가 보이세요?
손님	지금 광화문역 이(2) 번 출구 앞에 있어요. 여기에 서점과 약국이 있어요. 약국 앞에 횡단보도도 있어요.
준기	일단 횡단보도를 건너가세요. 그리고 왼쪽으로 가세요. 백 미터 쯤 걸어가시면 사거리가 있어요.
손님	네! 사거리에 있어요.
준기	사거리 건너편에 미용실이 보이세요? 미용실 이름은 뽀글뽀글이에요.
손님	네! 뽀글뽀글 미용실 앞에 있어요.
준기	식당은 미용실 근처에 있어요. 미용실 앞에서 오른쪽으로 가세요. 오십 미터 쯤 가시면 영화관이 있어요. 그리고 영화관 옆에 우리 식당이 있어요. 아리랑 식당이 보이세요?
손님	아 네! 아리랑 식당! 고맙습니다. *(enters shop)* 안녕하세요
준기	어서오세요! 몇 분이세요?

6 Read or listen to the conversation again and answer these questions.

  a Where is the customer calling from? What buildings can he see?
  b What are the first instructions that Junki gives?
  c What is the name of the hair salon Junki mentions?
  d How far do you need to walk from the hair salon to the restaurant?
  e What building is the restaurant next to?

7 Can you translate the following into English?

  a 지금 뭐가 보이세요?
  b 지금 광화문역 이 번 출구 앞에 있어요.
  c 약국 옆에 횡단보도도 있어요.
  d 왼쪽으로 가세요. 백 미터 쯤 걸어가시면 사거리가 있어요.
  e 식당은 미용실 근처에 있어요.
  f 영화관 옆에 우리 식당이 있어요. 아리랑이 보이세요?

Language discovery

 Complete the sentences with words from the box. Look at the conversations if necessary.

> -에   -에서   -으로   -면

a 근처 _____ 은행이 있어요?
b 저쪽 _____ 백 미터 쯤 걸어가시 _____ 거기 _____ 은행이 있어요.
c 미용실 앞 _____ 오른쪽 _____ 가세요.

1 -에 있어요: 'IT IS (AT/ON) . . .'

-에 있어요 is used after a location word to state or ask if someone or something is at that location. For example, 약국 옆에 있어요 translates as *It is next to the pharmacy*. The particle -에 is used as a marker of location.

2 -에서: 'AT, IN'

The particle -에서 is used as a particle of location, like the words *at* or *in* in English which express destinations or points of origin from which actions or movements take place. For example, 사거리에서 왼쪽으로 가세요 translates to *Turn left at the crossroad*. It is often abbreviated to -서 in colloquial speech; for example, 여기서 건너가세요 and 여기에서 건너가세요 can be used interchangeably to mean *Cross here*.

3 -(으)로: 'TO THE DIRECTION OF, TOWARD'

This particle indicates a direction, like *to the direction of* or *toward* in English. It follows a directional noun and its exact form varies between -으로 and -로 depending on the preceding noun's final syllable. For example, 저 쪽으로 is literally *to the direction of that side* which translates more naturally into *in that direction*. Likewise, 왼쪽으로 can be translated as *to the left* or *towards the left*.

4 -(으)면: 'IF'

This verb ending indicates condition. It is used to show that something will occur provided that something else happens – its basic meaning is *if*.

▶ -으면 is used for verb stems ending in consonants.
▶ -면 is used for those ending in vowels.

Practice

1 **Translate the sentences into English.**

a 이 쪽으로 똑바로 가세요.

b 저기 신호등 뒤에 은행이 있어요. 은행 옆에 미장원이 있어요.

c 지하철 역 삼(3) 번 출구 앞에 신호등이 있어요. 신호등 옆에 우체국 보이세요? 우체국으로 가세요.

d 여기서 횡단보도를 건너가시면 약국이 있어요. 약국에서 왼쪽으로 가세요.

e 근처에 병원이 없어요. 약국은 있어요. 저 쪽으로 이백 미터 쯤 걸어가시면 지하철 역 건너편에 약국이 있어요.

f 거기에 미용실도 있어요?

2 <u>06.05</u> **Say the following sentences out loud in Korean then listen and check your answers.**

a Ask if there is a department store in the area. Ask where it is.

b Ask a passer-by if they can see the cinema over there. Then ask if there is a bank next to the cinema. Ask if it is Seoul Bank.

c Ask where the bookstore is. Ask if there is a supermarket near the bookstore.

d Say if one turns left and walks about 100 metres there is a post office.

e Say there isn't a pharmacy nearby.

f Say from the hospital if one turns right and walks about 50 metres there is a crossroad and traffic lights.

g Say there is a hair salon on the left of the school. Say there is also a cinema behind the hair salon.

h Say the hospital is next to exit number 2 of Gangnam subway station.

3 **Complete the sentences with the correct word or ending from the box.**

> ·에   ·에서   -(으)면   -(으)로

a 여기서 오른쪽 _____ 가세요. 그리고 저기 횡단보도를 건너가시 _____ 슈퍼마켓이 있어요. 하나 슈퍼마켓이에요.

b 지하철 역 근처 _____ 약국이 있어요. 저기 병원 옆 _____ 역이 보이세요?

c 서 쪽 _____ 걸어가시 _____ 신호등 옆 _____ 학교가 있어요. 학교 _____ 왼쪽 _____ 가세요. 백 미터 쯤 가시 _____ 거기 _____ 미용실이 있어요.

4 You have agreed to run an errand for a colleague but cannot find the way to the bookstore. You call your colleague to ask for directions. Complete the conversation. Use the English prompts to help you.

Colleague	지금 어디에 있어요?
You	*Say you are in front of exit number 5 of the subway station.*
Colleague	오른쪽에 미용실 보이세요?
You	*Say yes. Then ask where the bookstore is. Ask if it is next to the hair salon.*
Colleague	아니에요. 서점은 은행과 약국 사이에 있어요.
You	*Ask where the bank is then.*
Colleague	은행은 여기서 똑바로 걸어가시면 횡단보도 앞에 있어요.
You	*Ask if there is a post office near the book store.*
Colleague	네! 우체국 있어요. 우체국은 약국 뒤에 있어요.
You	*Say thank you and goodbye.*

 5 You are stopped by a tourist trying to get to the department store. Offer her directions. Complete the conversation. Use the English prompts to help you.

Tourist	실례합니다.근처에 백화점이 어디에 있어요?
You	*Say the department store is in between exit number 4 of the subway station and the bookstore.*
Tourist	서점이 어디에 있어요?
You	*Tell the tourist to cross the zebra crossing over there. Then tell them if they turn right and walk about 200 metres, there will be a bookstore there.*
Tourist	백화점 근처에 은행도 있어요?
You	*Say yes, there is a bank near the department store. Say it is called Seoul Bank. Tell the tourist to turn left from the department store.*
Tourist	은행 옆에 뭐가 있어요?
You	*Say there is a pharmacy and school on the left of the bank and traffic lights across from the bank.*
Tourist	고맙습니다! 안녕히 가세요.

Speaking and listening

1 <u>06.06</u> **Listen to the conversation between the two strangers. Then read the statements and answer true or false.**

   a The bookstore is located behind the hospital.
   b The post office is located in front of the bookstore.
   c The bookstore is visible from where the gentleman is currently standing.
   d The gentleman needs to turn right to get to the bookstore.
   e The bookstore is roughly 300 metres away.
   f There is a bank located across from the bookstore.
   g There isn't a department store in the area, but there is a supermarket.
   h Hana Supermarket is about 200 metres away from the hospital.
   i There is a crossroad behind the traffic lights.
   j The supermarket is located behind the crossroad.
   k There is a hair salon in the area in between the school and hospital.

2 **Listen to the conversation again and take turns speaking each person's part.**

3 <u>06.07</u> **Listen to students talk about what they see around them. Match the names to the locations.**

   a Martin   **c** Billy
   b Susan   **d** Tanya

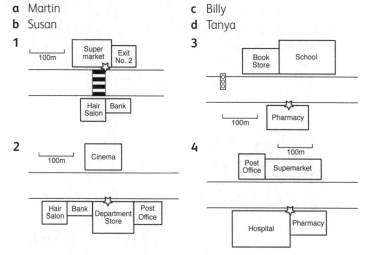

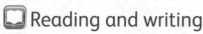

Reading and writing

1 You are meeting Jongmin for lunch. He sends you the following text, giving you directions to a restaurant. Read the text, then look at the map and choose the letter that best describes the restaurant's location.

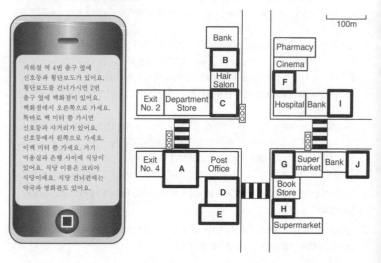

지하철 역 4번 출구 옆에 신호등과 횡단보도가 있어요. 횡단보도를 건너가시면 2번 출구 옆에 백화점이 있어요. 백화점에서 오른쪽으로 가세요. 똑바로 백 미터 쯤 가시면 신호등과 사거리가 있어요. 신호등에서 왼쪽으로 가세요. 이백 미터 쯤 가세요. 거기 미용실과 은행 사이에 식당이 있어요. 식당 이름은 코리아 식당이에요. 식당 건너편에는 약국과 영화관도 있어요.

2 You are hosting a party and send out directions with the invitations so that guests do not get lost on their way to the restaurant. Using the map, give directions to your guests.

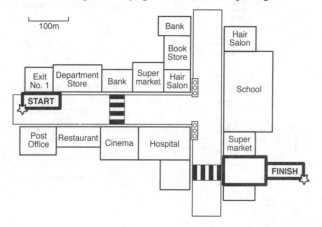

Test yourself

1 How would you do the following?

   a Say 'Excuse me' and ask if there is a cinema nearby. Then ask where it is.

   _____

   b Ask if one can see the hospital over there and the pharmacy next to it.

   _____

   c Say the hair salon is located between the department store and bank. Also say there is a zebra crossing and traffic lights in front of the hair salon.

   _____

   d Say if one walks about 350 metres in this direction, there is a school.

   _____

2 Match the particles and location words.

   a -(으)로   **1** at/in

   b -에   **2** to the direction of/toward

   c -에서   **3** (It is . . .) at/on

3 What verb ending means _if_? How does the form change depending on the preceding word's final letter?

4 Translate the following expressions into English.

   a 오른쪽에   **e** 왼쪽으로

   b 학교에서   **f** 거기에서

   c 저쪽으로   **g** 건너가시면

   d 걸어가시면   **h** 건너편에

SELF CHECK

I CAN...
. . . ask where a point of interest is located.
. . . ask for directions to a certain point of interest.
. . . describe the exact location of a point of interest.
. . . describe the way to a destination.

Review

1 **Complete the sentences and lists with an appropriate particle or word meaning. More than one answer may be possible.**

   a 사과 i _____ 배 ii _____ 오렌지 주세요. 영수증
      iii _____ 주세요.

   b 물 한 병 i _____ 과자 한 봉지 주세요. ii _____ 라면 한
      봉지 주세요.

   c 비빔밥 일 인분 i _____ 갈비 사 이분 주세요.
      ii _____ 맥주 두 병이요.

   d 저는 된장찌개 i _____ 불고기를 먹을래요. 비빔밥
      ii _____ 먹을게요.

   e 녹차 두 잔 i _____ 맥주 한 병 주세요. ii _____ 물 세 잔
      주세요.

2 **Translate the sentences into English. Pay attention to how you express the underlined particles.**

   a 왼쪽<u>으로</u> 가세요. 학교 옆<u>에</u> 약국이 있어요.

   b 이쪽<u>으로</u> 백 미터쯤 걸어가<u>면</u> 식당이 있어요.

   c 학교 앞<u>에서</u> 오른쪽<u>으로</u> 가세요.

   d 지하철 이 번 출구와 병원 사이<u>에</u> 영화관이 있어요.

   e 횡단보도를 건너가시<u>면</u> 식당 옆<u>에</u> 백화점이 있어요.

3 **Match the sentences in Korean to the English translations. Look at the verb endings for clues. There are two extra English translations. What are their Korean equivalents?**

   a 비빔밥 먹<u>을까요</u>? 저는 비빔밥을 먹을래요.

   b 비빔밥 먹<u>을게요</u>. 비빔밥 주세요.

   c 음료수 주문하<u>시겠어요</u>? 녹차와 물 있어요.

   d 저는 갈비를 먹<u>을게요</u>. 그리고 김치찌개도 먹<u>을래요</u>.

   i   I will eat bibimbap. Please give me bibimbap.

   ii Would you like to order drinks? We have green tea and water.

   iii Shall we eat bibimbap? I want to eat bibimbap.

   iv I will eat ribs. I want to eat kimchi stew, too.

   v   Shall we eat bibimbap? I will eat bibimbap.

   vi I want to eat ribs. I will eat kimchi stew too.

4 Put the prices in full in Korean. Be sure to use the appropriate number system!

a 15,038 won _____   **e** 6,280 won _____

b 5,400 won _____   **f** 99,999 won _____

c 290,600 won _____   **g** 3,845,020 won _____

d 47,100 won _____   **h** 7,420,380 won _____

5 Read the Korean expressions then put each into number form. Identify the number system.

a 예순둘 _____   (Pure/Sino-Korean)

b 사십오 _____   (Pure/Sino-Korean)

c 칠십구 _____   (Pure/Sino-Korean)

d 마흔다섯 _____   (Pure/Sino-Korean)

e 열일곱 _____   (Pure/Sino-Korean)

f 구십삼 _____   (Pure/Sino-Korean)

g 아흔아홉 _____   (Pure/Sino-Korean)

h 사십삼 _____   (Pure/Sino-Korean)

i 팔십팔 _____   (Pure/Sino-Korean)

6 Put the numbers in full in Korean. Note the counters in parentheses and choose the appropriate number system.

a _____ 50 인분 (portions)

b _____ 26 권 (books)

c _____ 19 병 (bottles)

d _____ 31 잔 (glasses)

e _____ 6 가지 (kinds)

f _____ 85,070 원 (won)

g _____ 7 개 (basic counting unit)

7 Somi is calling up to order a takeaway. She is planning to collect the order in person. She asks Taksu, the owner, for directions to the restaurant. Read their conversation and answer the questions that follow.

탁수	안녕하세요 아리랑 식당이에요. 주문하시겠어요?
소미	안녕하세요. 비빔밥 일 인분과 불고기 이 인분 주문할게요.
탁수	비빔밥 일 인분과 불고기 이 인분이요.
소미	그리고 된장 찌개 있어요? 된장 찌개도 주세요.
탁수	죄송해요 된장 찌개 없어요. 김치찌개는 있어요.
소미	그럼 김치찌개 주세요.
탁수	김치찌개 몇 인분 주문하시겠어요?
소미	이 인분 주세요. 모두 얼마예요?
탁수	모두 삼만육천원이에요.
소미	네. 그리고 식당은 어디에 있어요?
탁수	하나 슈퍼마켓과 도레미 약국 사이에 있어요.
소미	도레미 약국이요? 도레미 약국은 어디에 있어요?
탁수	지하철 역 근처에 있어요. 압구정 역 삼 번 출구에서 왼쪽으로 가세요. 그리고 병원 앞 횡단보도를 건너 가시면 영화관이 있어요. 거기서 왼쪽으로 오십 미터 쯤 가시면 도레미 약국이 있어요.
소미	네 고맙습니다.

a What is Taksu's restaurant called?

b What meat dish does Somi order? How many portions?

c What dish does Somi ask for that Taksu doesn't sell? What does he sell instead?

d How many kinds of dishes does Somi order in total? What are they?

e How much is the final bill?

f The restaurant is located between Hana department store and Do-Re-Mi pharmacy. True or False?

g Does Somi know where Do-Re-Mi pharmacy is?

h Which sentence in the conversation means: 'From exit number 3 of Apgujeong station, turn left'?

i Where is the cinema located in relation to the hospital?

j Roughly how far away is the Do-Re-Mi pharmacy from the cinema?

8 Somi is to do a short review on Arirang restaurant and its food, but she is sick. Read the following reviews on other restaurants in Apgujeong and then do Somi's review for her.

EXTRA USEFUL VOCABULARY

비싸요.	*It's expensive.*
하지만	*but*
싸요.	*It's cheap.*
맛이 없어요.	*It's not tasty.*

서라벌 식당

서라벌은 김치찌개가 정말 맛있어요. 그런데 조금 매워요. 갈비도 맛있어요! 그리고 싸요!서라벌 식당은 압구정 역 근처에 있어요.압구정 역 오 번 출구에서 오른쪽으로 100 미터 쯤 가시면 식당이 있어요.

아사달 식당

아사달 식당은 너무 비싸요. 된장찌개와 불고기는 너무 짜요. 그리고 비빔밥은 맛이 없어요. 정말 맛이 없어요. 식당은 압구정 역 뒤 서점 옆에 있어요.

---

9 Hyemi is doing her weekly grocery shopping. Read her conversation with the shop assistant Martin and list all the items she buys, as well as the quantity of each. How much does it all cost her?

마틴	안녕하세요. 어서오세요!
혜미	안녕하세요. 주스하고 우유 있어요?
마틴	네 주스는 오렌지 주스가 있고, 우유는 딸기와 초코, 두 가지가 있어요.
혜미	오렌지 주스 두 병하고 딸기 우유 한 개 주세요. 그리고 사과 주세요!
마틴	사과는 없어요. 죄송해요. 하지만 배는 있어요.
혜미	그럼 빵은 있어요?
마틴	네. 크림빵과 단팥빵 있어요.
혜미	얼마예요?
마틴	크림빵은 한 개에 팔백원이고 단팥빵은 한 개에 칠백오십원이에요.
혜미	그럼 크림빵 한개와 단팥빵 세 개 주세요!
마틴	네. 모두 오천사백오십원이에요.
혜미	아 그리고 영수증노 주세요.
마틴	네 여기 있어요. 고맙습니다. 안녕히 가세요!
혜미	고맙습니다. 안녕히 계세요.

7 교통.
강남에 어떻게 가요?

Transport. How do I get to Gangnam?

In this unit, you will learn how to:
▶ *describe a route by transport*
▶ *explain and compare ways to get to a destination.*
▶ *state the time it takes going from one place to another.*

CEFR: *(A2) Can understand and give instructions for travelling via various modes of transport to reach a destination. (A1) Can recognize and use basic phrases to compare different routes and state the time it takes.*

📷 Transport

대중 교통 (*public transport*) in Korea is first class. The 지하철 (*subway*) network, found in six major cities, combined with the extensive 버스 (*bus*) and 기차 (*train, rail*) systems, make getting around the country very easy, efficient and affordable.

The nation's capital 서울 (*Seoul*) in particular, with more than 10 million residents, has well-developed routes that are conveniently connected to most 공공 건물 (*public buildings*), 유적지 (*places of historic interest*), 쇼핑몰 (*shopping malls*) and other popular 관광지 (*tourist attractions*).

If using a 교통 카드 (*transportation card*), you can get 환승 할인 (*transfer discount*) on your journeys when transferring from one 버스 or 지하철 to the next. Make sure to beep your 교통 카드 each time when getting off, as well as getting on, to get your 환승 할인!

Travelling by 택시 (*taxi*) in Korea is reasonably inexpensive and another popular form of 교통 (*transport*). Most taxis now also provide 동시통역 (*simultaneous interpretation*) services on the 전화 (*phone*), making them very foreigner friendly. However, Seoul's 도로 (*roads*) are always heavily congested so do be aware of this.

How many types of 대중 교통 are mentioned in the text? Are they as popular in your local city too?

Vocabulary builder

<u>07.01</u> **Read the vocabulary and try to pronounce each word. Then listen and try to imitate the speakers.**

TRANSPORT

자동차	*car*
(-번) 버스	*bus (number -)*
택시	*taxi*
(-호선) 지하철	*subway (line number -)*
기차	*train*
자전거	*bicycle*
오토바이	*motorbike*
버스 정류장	*bus stop*
.... 역	*. . . station*

NEW EXPRESSIONS

. . . 에 어떻게 가요?	*How do I get to . . . ?*
. . . 에 가고 싶어요.	*I want to go to . . .*
. . . (으)로 갈 수 있어요.	*You can go by . . .*
. . . (으)로 가야 돼요.	*You have to go by . . .*
. . . 가는 - 있어요?	*Is there a - going to/bound for . . . ?*
. . . 에서 - 을/를 타세요.	*Get on the . . .*
. . . 에서 - (으)로 갈아타세요.	*Transfer . . .*
. . . 에서 내리세요.	*Get off . . .*
갈아타야 돼요.	*You have to transfer.*
- 에서 . . . 까지	*from - to . . .*
얼마나 걸려요?	*How long does it take?*
제일	*most*
-보다 더	*more . . . than*
-(이)나	*or*
밖에	*only*
빨라요, 느려요	*it is fast, it is slow*
멀어요, 가까워요	*it is far away, it is close*

 # Conversations

07.02 *Taehee wants to go to Gangnam. A passer-by describes how to get there. Listen and answer the questions.*

1 Which mode of transport is the fastest?

태희	실례합니다. 강남에 가고 싶어요. 어떻게 가요?
행인	잠실 지하철 역에서 이(2) 호선을 타세요. 그리고 강남 역에서 내리세요.
태희	잠실 역이 어디에 있어요?
행인	저기 식당 보이세요? 식당 앞에 오(5) 번 출구가 있어요.
태희	강남 역 가는 버스 있어요?
행인	오(5) 번 출구 옆에 버스 정류장이 있어요. 거기서 삼백육십번 버스가 강남으로 가요. 하지만 지하철이 제일 빨라요.
태희	멀어요? 잠실 역에서 강남 역까지 얼마나 걸려요?
행인	아니요. 가까워요. 십오분 쯤 걸려요.

2 Read or listen to the conversation again and answer these questions.

   a If Taehee wants to takes the subway, which line must she take?

   b At which station must she get the subway? Where is this station located?

   c Which number bus will take Taehee to Gangnam?

   d How long does the passer-by think it will take to get to Gangnam?

3 Can you say the following in Korean?

   a I want to go to Busan. How do I get there?

   b And get off at Busan station.

   c Is there a bus that goes to the Busan area?

   d However, the train is the fastest.

   e Is it far away? How long does it take from Gangnam station to Busan station?

   f Yes. It is far away. It takes roughly 30 minutes.

 4 07.03 Taehee stops you to ask for directions to Oksu subway station. Tell her how to get to her destination. Use the English prompts to help you.

Sarah is asking Jinu, a guide at the tourism office, how to get to several different places. Listen and answer the questions.

5 How many places does Sarah get directions for?

사라	오늘 동대문 시장에 가야 돼요. 어떻게 가요?
진우	지하철을 타야 돼요. 저기 경복궁 역에서 삼(3)호선을 타세요.
사라	갈아타야 돼요?
진우	네 갈아타야 돼요! 종로삼(3)가 역에서 일(1)호선으로 갈아타세요. 그리고 동대문 역에서 내리세요.
사라	동대문 시장 가는 버스도 있어요?
진우	아니요. 버스 없어요. 지하철 밖에 없어요.
사라	그럼 남대문 시장에 어떻게 가요?
진우	버스나 지하철로 갈 수 있어요. 택시도 있어요. 남대문 시장은 조금 멀어요. 버스나 지하철보다 택시가 더 빨라요.
사라	그리고 내일 부산 가고 싶어요. 부산에 어떻게 가요?
진우	기차로 가세요. 세 시간 쯤 걸려요.

6 Read or listen to the conversation again and answer these questions.

　　a Which lines must Sarah take to get to Dongdaemun market? At which stations must she get on, transfer and get off the subway?

　　b Which three modes of transport can Sarah choose from to get to Namdaemun market? Which is the fastest?

　　c Where does Sarah want to go tomorrow and what mode of transport should she take? Roughly how long will it take?

7 Can you translate the following into English?

　　a 종로삼가 역에서 일 호선으로 갈아타세요. 그리고 동대문 역에서 내리세요.

　　b 버스 없어요. 지하철 밖에 없어요.

　　c 조금 멀어요. 버스나 지하철보다 택시가 더 빨라요.

8 Give the number system used for the following, using information in both conversations.

　　a 호선 (subway line)　　　**c** 번 (bus number)

　　b 시간 (hours – as a period of time)　　**d** 분 (minutes)

Language discovery

 Find these sentences in the conversations. Did you notice the new verb endings?

a I want to go to Gangnam.

b You can go by bus or subway.

c You have to take the subway. You have to transfer.

1 'WANT TO DO SOMETHING': -고 싶어요

-고 싶어요 is another ending that expresses your want, wish or desire to do something. It can only be used when talking about yourself or the person you are talking to. For example the phrase I _want_ to get off becomes 내리고 싶어요, using the verb stem 내리- meaning _to get off_. Similarly the sentence I _want_ to go to school in Korean is 학교에 가고 싶어요, using the stem 가- meaning _to go_.

2 'CAN DO SOMETHING': -(으)ㄹ 수 있어요

-(으)ㄹ 수 있어요 translates as _can_.

▶ -을 수 있어요 is used after verb stems ending in a consonant.

▶ -ㄹ 수 있어요 is used for stems ending in a vowel.

Using the verb stem 가- for the verb _to go_, the sentence I _can_ go to school becomes 학교에 갈 수 있어요. The same ending but with 없어요 instead of 있어요 translates as _cannot_, 학교에 갈 수 없어요 translates to I _cannot_ go to school.

3 'MUST DO SOMETHING': -어/아/여야 돼요

-아/어야 돼요 is attached to a verb stem to express obligation and most typically translates as _have to_ or _must_. For example, the sentences 여기서 갈아타야 돼요 and 버스로 가야 돼요 mean You _must_ transfer here and You _have to_ go by bus.

▶ If the final vowel of the verb stem is ㅏ or ㅗ, -아야 돼요 is used.

▶ For all final vowels other than ㅏ or ㅗ, -어야 돼요 is used.

▶ For stems ending in 하-, -여야 돼요 is used and normally contracted to 해야 돼요.

Note: This is very similar to constructing -요 ending forms of various verbs which will be covered more extensively in Unit 9.

Complete the sentences with words from the box. Look at the conversations if necessary.

| -에서 | -까지 | -보다 더 | -나 | -로 | 밖에 |

a 버스 _____ 지하철 _____ 갈 수 있어요. 버스나 지하철
_____ 택시가 빨라요.

b 잠실 역 _____ 강남 역 _____ 얼마나 걸려요?

c 지하철 _____ 없어요.

4 'FROM - TO': -에서 -까지

As a single particle -에서 means *at* or *in*. However, when used with -까지, the construction means *from . . . to . . .*: 서울<u>에서</u> 부산<u>까지</u> becomes *from Seoul to Busan*. It is used after place nouns and describes the starting point and destination.

5 'MORE THAN': -보다 더

-보다 더 is used to mean *more than* in comparative sentences. -보다 더 attaches to the noun to which the subject is being compared. For example, in the sentence 기차가 자동차<u>보다 더</u> 빨라요 (*The train is faster than the car*), the particle attaches to *car*, which the train is being compared to.

6 'OR': -(이)나

-이나 is used following a consonant and -나 is used after a vowel. This particle is used to express choice between two nouns in a similar way to *or* in English. For example 택시<u>나</u> 기차를 타세요 translates into *Get on a taxi or train*.

7 'ONLY': 밖에

Though not strictly a particle, 밖에 operates like a particle in that it adds the meaning of *only* to the noun that it follows. 밖에 must always appear with a negative verb such as 없어요: 택시 <u>밖에</u> 없어요 (*There are only taxis*).

8 'VIA, BY': -(으)로

Meaning *by* or *via*, -로 follows a noun ending in a vowel or ㄹ, while -으로 is used after all consonants other than ㄹ. 기차<u>로</u> 가세요 translates into *Go by train*.

ℹ️ Practice

1 **Complete the sentences with verb endings and particles introduced in this unit.**

a 약국에 _____ (*have to go*, stem: 가-). 택시를 _____ (*want to get on*, stem: 타-). 택시가 버스 _____ (*than*) 빨라요.

b 부산에 기차 _____ (*or*) 버스 _____ (*by*) _____ (*can go*, stem; 가-).

c 교대에서 _____ (*can transfer*, stem: 갈아타-). 광화문 _____ (*from*) 교대_____ (*to*) 삼십분 쯤 걸려요.

d 여기 정류장에서 버스를 _____ (*have to get on*, stem: 타-). 버스 _____ (*only*) 없어요. 시청 가는 지하철이 없어요.

2 **Translate the following into English?**

a 오토바이로 갈 수 있어요. 오토바이가 자동차보다 더 빨라요. 제일 빨라요.

b 지하철 밖에 없어요. 강남(으로) 가는 버스가 없어요. 너무 멀어요.

c 내일 백화점에 가야 돼요. 택시나 자동차 타고 싶어요.

d 기차로 가면 서울에서 부산까지 세 시간 쯤 걸려요.

e 충무로에서 삼(3) 호선으로 갈아타야 돼요. 그럼 안국 역에 갈 수 있어요.

f 여기서 내리고 싶어요. 저기 약국에 가야 돼요.

 3 <u>07.05</u> **Say your answers out loud then listen and check your answers.**

a Say you want to go to Hana supermarket. Ask how you get there.

b Say you have to go to Busan. Ask if there is a subway bound for Seoul station.

c Say one can go to Gangnam by subway or bus. Then say 'but a taxi is faster than the subway or bus'.

d Ask how to get to Apgujeong. Ask if one can go by bicycle.

e Tell a passer-by to get on bus number 1300 at the bus stop over there. Then tell them to get off in front of Sinchon station.

f Tell a passer-by to get on the subway, line number 4. Then tell them they can transfer at Yongsan. Say there is no bus, there is only the subway.

g Say one has to transfer to line 8 at Jamsil station. Also say one must get off at Cheonho station. Then say it takes approximately 20 minutes.

h Say the car is faster than the bus. Then say, but the car is slower than the train.

i Say you have to go to the bus stop. Ask how you must get there.

Speaking

You are working at the tourism office and a tourist asks how to get some attractions. Offer him assistance. Complete the conversation using the English prompts for guidance.

Tourist 안녕하세요. 로데오 거리에 가고 싶어요. 어떻게 가야 돼요?

You *Say you have to go by subway. Tell him to get on line 3 and get off at Apgujeong station. Then say you have to walk. Say from the station to Rodeo Road it takes roughly 10 minutes.*

Tourist 그리고 경복궁에는 어떻게 가요?

You *Say you can get a bus or subway, but the subway is faster. Tell him to get on line 3 and get off at Gyeongbokkung station.*

Tourist 그럼 남산 타워는 어떻게 가요?

You *Say you have to take line 3 and then transfer to line 4 at Chungmuro. Tell him to get off at Myeongdong station and to get on a taxi in front of exit number 3.*

Tourist 정말 고맙습니다! 안녕히 계세요.

Listening

<u>07.06</u> Listen to the conversation between Sarah and Jinu, the tourism office assistant, and then answer the questions.

a Which number buses go to the 63 Building? Is the bus the fastest route?

b If Sarah takes the subway to the 63 Building, at which station and exit number should she transfer to the number 62 bus?

c Which subway lines must Sarah take to go to Lotte World? At which stations must she get on, transfer and get off? How long does it take roughly?

d Are there any buses going to Lotte World?

e Which is further away – 63 Building or Lotte World?

f Can Sarah go to Itaewon via bus? Is this the recommended route? Why? Describe the complete route Jinu recommends to Sarah.

g Which mode of transportation is best to get to Deoksugung Palace? Why?

h Which subway lines take you to the palace? Which station do you get off at?

i How do you travel from the subway station onwards? How long does it take roughly?

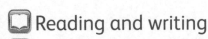

Reading and writing

1 Jinu explains how he gets from home to work every morning. Read the passage below and answer the questions.

회사에서 우리 집은 멀어요. 집에서 회사까지 한 시간 쯤 걸려요. 집 앞에서 십번이나 십오번 버스를 타요. 그리고 동대문 시장 근처에서 내려요. 동대문 역에서 지하철로 갈아타요. 동대문 역에는 사호선과 일호선이 있어요. 일호선을 타면 종로 삼가에서 삼호선으로 갈아탈 수 있어요. 회사는 옥수 역 근처에 있어요. 그래서 삼호선을 타야 돼요. 옥수 역에서 내리면 이 번 출구 뒤에 회사가 있어요. 옥수로 가는 버스도 있어요. 하지만 지하철이 버스보다 더 빨라요. 버스 타면 느려요.

  a How long does it take approximately for Jinu to get from home to work?
  b Which mode of transport does he take first?
  c At which station does he get on the subway?
  d Where is his final destination? Which subway line is this station on?
  e Where exactly is Jinu's office located in relation to the subway station?
  f What alternative mode of transportation can Jinu take? Why doesn't he?
  g Are the following statements true or false?
    1 The buses number 12 and 15 stop outside Jinu's house.
    2 Subway lines 1 and 5 stop at Dongdaemun station.
    3 Subway lines 1 and 3 stop at Jongno 3-ga.
    4 Subway line number 3 stops at Oksu.

2 Write a passage about yourself. How do you get from home to work or school every day?

3 Minji and Jihoon want to visit the Korean Folk Village, but they are travelling from different places and don't know the way. Use these routes and give directions to each of them.

민지: 서울역 ⟶ (train bound for Suwon, 30 mins) ⟶ 수원역

수원역 ⟶ (bus 37 outside subway exit 4, 20 mins) ⟶ 한국 민속촌

지훈: 신사역 ⟶ (subway line 3) ⟶ 서울대입구역 ⟶ (transfer to line 2) ⟶ 강남역

강남역 ⟶ (bus 560 outside subway exit 6, 50 mins) ⟶ 한국 민속촌

Test yourself

1 How would you do the following?

   a Say you want to go to Dogok. Ask how you get there and if you can go by train.

   _____

   b Ask if there is a bus from this bus stop that goes to Sinchon.

   _____

   c Say you have to get on line 8 at Jamsil station and then you can transfer at Cheonho to line 5. Say you have to get off at the Olympic Park.

   _____

   d Say you have to get on the train or subway. Say there is also a bus but Suwon station is far away. The train and subway are faster than the bus.

   _____

2 Give the English definition of these verb endings.

   a -고 싶어요   **b** -(으)ㄹ 수 있어요   **c** -어/아/여야 돼요

3 What particle corresponds to these words?

   a via, by   **b** only   **c** more . . . than   **d** from . . . to . . .   **e** or

4 Translate the sentences into English.

   a 자동차나 택시   **f** 자동차로 가고 싶어요.
   b 기차 밖에 없어요.   **g** 거기에서 내려야 돼요.
   c 서울역에서 강남까지   **h** 안국에서 갈아타야 돼요.
   d 자전거보다 더 빨라요. **i** 일호선으로 갈아타세요.
   e 버스로 갈 수 있어요.

SELF CHECK

	I CAN...
○	. . . ask how to get to a destination using various modes of transport.
○	. . . give instructions to get to a destination using various modes of transport.
○	. . . compare different routes to the same destination.
○	. . . state the time it takes getting from one place to another.

8 취미가 뭐예요?

What are your hobbies?

In this unit, you will learn how to:
▶ *state your hobbies and give reasons you like them.*
▶ *list activities that you like and dislike.*
▶ *state the frequency that you do such activities.*

CEFR: *(A1) Can recognize and use basic phrases to list hobbies, likes and dislikes. (A1) Can understand simple expressions to describe the frequency one does a hobby or sport.*

Hobbies and pastimes

운동 (*sports*) is a very popular 취미 (*hobby*) in Korea. In addition to traditional martial arts 태권도 (*taekwondo*) and folk wrestling 씨름 (*ssirum*), all modern sports are widely enjoyed. In particular, 축구 (*football*), 농구 (*basketball*), 야구 (*baseball*) and 골프 (*golf*) are among the nation's favourites with notable 한국 선수 (*Korean athletes*) playing in teams all over the world. 박지성 (*JiSung Park*) was the first Asian to win Champions League Football, 박찬호 (*ChanHo Park*) became the first 한국사람 (*Korean person*) to play in major league baseball, and 박세리 (*SeRi Pak*) was the first Korean to win the LPGA Tour.

At least half of the south Korean peninsula is composed of mountains, making 등산 (*hiking*) another common pastime. Many choose to climb the mountains every morning to collect water from the 약수터 (*mineral springs*). Others may climb the mountains to visit 절 (*temples*) or to simply do a bit of exercise.

Recently, the increasing popularity of 컴퓨터 게임 (*computer games*) and 인터넷 게임 (*Internet games*) has created concerns that children aren't getting enough exercise. The easy access to 피씨방 (*Internet cafes*) and 게임방 (*gaming arcades*) means gaming 중독 (*addiction*) is becoming increasingly prevalent.

How many hobbies are listed in the text? Are these pastimes that you enjoy too? Are they popular in your area too?

Vocabulary builder

08.01 **Read the vocabulary and try to pronounce each word. Then listen and try to imitate the speakers.**

HOBBIES

음악을 들어요.	I listen to music.
그림을 그려요.	I draw pictures.
우표를 모아요.	I collect stamps.
책을 읽어요.	I read books.
여행을 해요.	I go travelling.
컴퓨터 게임을 해요.	I play computer games.
피아노 연습을 해요.	I practise the piano.
요리를 해요.	I cook.
사진을 찍어요.	I take photos.
운동 해요.	I do sports.
등산/낚시 … 해요.	I go … hiking/fishing.
축구/야구/농구 … 해요.	I play … football/baseball/basketball.
골프/테니스/탁구/배드민턴 … 쳐요	I play … golf/tennis/table tennis/ badminton.

NEW EXPRESSIONS

취미가 뭐예요?	What are your hobbies?
시간이 있을 때 무엇을 해요?	What do you do in your free time?
… 좋아해요? 왜 좋아해요?	Do you like … ? Why do you like it?
좋아해요/싫어해요 / 즐겨요	I like … /I dislike … /I enjoy …
재미있어요, 신나요	it is fun, it is exciting
건강에 좋아요, 건강해져요	it is good for one's health, you become fit
기분이 좋아져요, 스트레스가 풀려요	it makes me feel better, it relieves stress
힘들어요, 어려워요, 저랑 안 맞아요	it is tiring, it is difficult, it's not for me
재미없어요, 지루해요	it isn't fun, it is boring
얼마나 자주 운동해요?	How often do you play sports?
요즘, 보통, 자주, 가끔	these days, normally, often, sometimes
매일, 매주, 매달	every day, every week, every month
하루/이틀/며칠에 -번	- times a day/every two days/few days
일주일/한달/일년에 -번	- times a week/month/year

 Conversations

08.02 *Jongsu and Mikyung are discussing their hobbies. Listen and answer the questions.*

1 Who likes reading – Jongsu or Mikyung?

종수	미경씨, 취미가 뭐예요?
미경	제 취미는 책 읽는 것과 피아노 연습하는 것이에요. 종수씨는 취미가 뭐예요?
종수	저는 운동하는 것을 좋아해요!
미경	무슨 운동을 좋아해요?
종수	저는 축구와 농구를 제일 좋아해요! 등산하는 것도 즐겨요. 미경씨도 운동 좋아해요?
미경	네! 저도 등산하는 것을 즐겨요. 그리고 테니스도 자주 쳐요. 종수씨는 운동을 왜 좋아해요?
종수	재미있고 스트레스가 풀려요! 가끔 조금 힘들지만 좋아해요! 그럼 미경씨는 책 읽는 것을 왜 좋아해요?
미경	재밌어요! 저는 책 읽는 것이 정말 재밌어요.

2 Read or listen to the conversation again and answer these questions.

a What are Mikyung's hobbies? Does she say she enjoys travelling?

b Which sports does Jongsu like the most? Does he enjoy any others?

c Does Mikyung like sports? If so, which ones in particular?

d Why does Jongsu like sports? Why does Mikyung like reading?

3 Say the sentences in Korean.

a My hobbies are cooking and taking photos.

b I like badminton and tennis the most! I also enjoy fishing.

c I also often play baseball.

d Though it is sometimes very tiring I enjoy it!

 4 08.03 **Jongsu asks you about your hobbies. What do you do in your free time? Continue the conversation. Use the English prompts to help you.**

Jongsu and Minjun are discussing which sports they like. Listen and answer the questions.

5 Do Jongsu and Minjun like sports?

종수	민준씨, 취미가 뭐예요? 운동 좋아해요?
민준	제 취미는 운동이에요! 네 운동 정말 좋아해요!
종수	저도 운동 좋아해요! 민준씨는 무슨 운동 좋아해요?
민준	저는 야구를 제일 좋아해요. 탁구도 자주 쳐요. 그리고 한 달에 한 번 등산을 해요! 종수씨는 무슨 운동을 좋아해요?
종수	저는 배드민턴을 제일 좋아해요! 낚시와 골프도 즐겨요.
민준	배드민턴은 얼마나 자주 쳐요?
종수	요즘 배드민턴은 매일 쳐요! 하지만 보통 이틀에 한 번 쳐요.
민준	낚시는 얼마나 자주 해요?
종수	한 달에 다섯 번 쯤 해요! 낚시가 정말 재밌어요. 낚시하면 기분이 좋아져요. 민준씨는 야구 자주 해요?
민준	네 매주 목요일과 토요일에 야구 해요. 건강에 정말 좋아요.

6 Read or listen to the conversation again and answer these questions.

a Which sport does Minjun like the most? How often does he play and why does he like it so much?

b What other sports does Minjun play? How often?

c What is Jongsu's favourite sport? How often has he been playing lately? Is this more frequent than usual?

d What other sports does Jongsu enjoy?

e How often does Jongsu go fishing? Why does he like fishing?

7 Can you translate this into English?

a 저도 운동 좋아해요! 민준씨는 무슨 운동 좋아해요?

b 탁구도 자주 쳐요. 그리고 한 달에 한 번 등산을 해요!

c 배드민턴은 얼마나 자주 쳐요?

d 한 달에 다섯 번 쯤 해요! 낚시하면 기분이 좋아져요.

e 민준씨는 야구 자주 해요?

f 매주 목요일과 토요일에 야구 해요. 건강에 정말 좋아요.

Language discovery

**Find the Korean for the English sentences below in the first
conversation. Think about the additional examples: can you figure
out the verb endings that mean *and* and *though*?**

a It is fun and relieves stress! **b** Though it is sometimes a little
tiring I like it!

More examples:

건강에 좋고 신나요. *It is good for your health and exciting.*

지루하고 어려워요. *It is boring and difficult.*

신나고 재미있지만 너무 힘들어요. *Though it's exciting and fun it's
too difficult.*

스트레스가 풀리지만 저랑 안 맞아요. *Though it relieves stress it's not
for me.*

1 'AND': -고

-고 operates like *and* in English to link two sentences, in either the past,
present or future tense. -고 is attached to the verb stem in the first
sentence and the second sentence then follows on. This verb ending
can be used instead of the word for *also*, 그리고, that you learned in
earlier units.

For example, the two sentences 재미있어요. 그리고 스트레스가
풀려요! (*It is fun. Also it relieves stress.*) can become a single one by
replacing 그리고 with -고: 재미있고 스트레스가 풀려요! (*It is fun and
relieves stress!*).

2 'THOUGH': -지만

-지만 is used similarly to *though* in English. It is the most common
ending to mark contrast between two clauses or sentences. As with -고,
it is attached to the verb stem in the contrasting clause or sentence and
the other follows on. -지만 can be used instead of the word for *however*,
하지만, presented in earlier units.

For example, the two sentences 가끔 조금 힘들어요. 하지만 좋아해요!
(*It is sometimes a little tiring. However I like it!*) can become one by
replacing 하지만 with -지만: 가끔 조금 힘들<u>지만</u> 좋아해요! This
sentence will translate to <u>*Though*</u> *it is sometimes a little tiring I like it!* or
It is sometimes a little tiring <u>but</u> I like it!

One ending completes these expressions. Find it in the conversations then complete the sentences. Can you guess what it means?

   a 제 취미는 책 읽 _____ 과 피아노 연습 _____ 이에요.

   b 저는 운동 _____ 을 좋아해요!

   c 저는 축구와 농구를 제일 좋아해요! 등산 _____ 도 즐겨요.

3 '-ING': -는 것

The ending -는 것 is attached a verb stem to change the verb into a noun of -*ing* form. For example, 등산을 해요 (*I go hiking*) has the verb stem 등산하-. Attaching -는 것 gives 등산<u>하는 것</u>, meaning *go<u>ing</u> hiking*, or simply *hiking*.

Look at these frequency words in the second conversation. Go back and find them in Korean.

   a I go hiking once every month!

   b However, normally I play once every two days.

   c I go approximately five times every month!

   d Yes, I play baseball every week on Thursdays and Saturdays.

4 ' . . . TIMES A -': -에 . . . 번

This expression is attached to a noun which describes time or interval, and it is used to indicate how often one does something.

It is very similar to the pricing expression presented in Unit 4. Look at the examples below to see how it is used.

일주일에 한 번 운동 해요.	*I do sports once a week.*
한 달에 세 번 그림을 그려요.	*I draw pictures three times a month.*

5 'EVERY -': 매-

The word 매- in front of nouns indicating units of time is the equivalent of *every*. For example, when succeeded by 일 (*day*) to give 매일 it means *every day*; when succeeded by 주 (*week*) to form 매주, it means *every week*, and so forth.

Practice

1 **Complete the sentences using expressions from this unit. Where appropriate the verb stem is given as a clue.**

   a _____ (*every week*) 등산을 해요. _____ (*though it is tiring,* stem: 힘들-) 재미있어요.

   b 요즘에는 _____ (*five times a month*) 낚시 해요. _____ (*it makes me feel better* and, stem: 기분이 좋아지-) 스트레스가 풀려요. 저는 _____ (*fishing,* 낚시 하-)을 정말 좋아해요.

   c 축구를 보통 _____ (*every day*) 해요. 스트레스가 풀려요.

2 **Translate the sentences into English.**

   a 시간이 있을 때 무엇을 해요? 야구 좋아해요?

   b 매일 사진을 찍어요. 사진 찍는 것이 정말 재미있어요.

   c 이틀에 한 번 컴퓨터 게임을 해요. 재미있지만 어려워요.

   d 요즘 여행을 자주 해요. 신나고 기분이 좋아져요.

   e 배드민턴 치는 것을 즐겨요. 건강해져요. 그리고 스트레스가 풀려요.

   f 책 읽는 것을 즐기지만 음악 듣는 것을 제일 좋아해요.

   g 탁구 싫어해요. 힘들고 어려워요. 저랑 안 맞아요.

   h 운동 하는 것을 좋아해요. 건강해지고 신나요. 매주 운동 해요.

3 <u>08.05</u> **Say the following out loud then listen and check your answers.**

   a Say you read books every week. Say you also practise the piano every day.

   b Say you like playing golf. Say it relieves stress.

   c Say you collect stamps these days. Say you sometimes cook too.

   d Say you enjoy basketball. Say it's good for one's health and it is fun.

   e Say you dislike tennis. Say though it is exciting it is too tiring and difficult.

   f Say you play sports often. Say you play football once every two days. Then say you play golf two times a week.

   g Say you dislike fishing. Say it is boring and not fun.

   h Ask how often one plays sports. Ask if one likes basketball and baseball.

Speaking

Martin is asking you about your hobbies. He wants to know what you do in your free time. Answer his questions and ask him about his hobbies.

Martin	취미가 뭐예요?
You	*Say you like sports. Say you play table tennis and badminton.*
Martin	탁구는 왜 좋아해요?
You	*Say it is exciting and it relieves stress. Say it is also really fun!*
Martin	얼마나 자주 쳐요?
You	*Say you normally play every week. Say however these days you play three times a week.*
Martin	축구도 좋아해요?
You	*Say No, you don't like football.*
Martin	왜 싫어해요?
You	*Say it is not for you. Say that table tennis is more exciting than football. Also say football is too tiring.*

Listening

1 08.06 **Listen to the following people talk about their hobbies then complete the table. List the activities each person likes and dislikes.**

	Likes	Dislikes
Sarah	*badminton, tennis*	*reading*
a Mark		
b Andrew		
c Jane		
d Bella		

2 08.07 **Listen to Jiho and Suji's conversation and answer the questions.**

   a List Suji's hobbies. What does she enjoy doing the most? Why?
   b Does Suji like any sports? What does she think of sports in general?
   c Which sports does Jiho like? What does Jiho think of tennis?
   d How often does Jiho play football and basketball?

Reading and writing

1 Read the email from Minki and answer the questions.

마틴씨, 안녕하세요! 마틴씨는 취미가 뭐예요? 시간이 있을 때 무엇을 해요? 저는 운동을 싫어해요. 너무 힘들고 저랑 안 맞아요. 저는 운동 보다 책 읽는 것을 좋아해요. 그리고 여행 하는 것을 즐겨요. 재미있고 신나요! 일 년에 두번 쯤 여행을 해요. 영화 보는 것도 정말 좋아해요. 영화를 보면 기분이좋아져요! 저는 매주 영화를 봐요. 보통 한 달에 두 번 쯤 영화를 봐요. 그런데 요즘에는 매주 봐요! 마틴씨도 영화 좋 아해요?

   a What does Minki think of sports?
   b Which hobbies does Minki mention? Why does he like them?
   c Does he like watching films too? Why?
   d How often does he normally watch films? Does he watch more or less films these days?

2 Martin is having trouble understanding the Korean. Translate the email above for him into English.

3 Now reply to Minki's email as Martin. Address the email to Minki, put it in Korean and don't forget to answer the questions Minki asks.

Test yourself

1 How would you do the following?

a Ask what someone's hobbies are. Ask if s/he likes collecting stamps.

_____

b Say you enjoy playing golf and drawing pictures. Say it relieves stress.

_____

c Say you dislike sports. Though it is good for your health it is too tiring and boring.

_____

d Say you play baseball once every two days. Say it makes you feel better.

_____

e Say you normally like to cook and read books. However these days you practise the piano every day.

_____

2 Match the endings and functions.

a -는 것	**1**	connects two sentences with the meaning *and*
b -고	**2**	connects two sentences with the meaning *though*
c -지만	**3**	*-ing*, changes a verb to a noun

3 Translate the following frequency expressions.

a 매주 일요일   **e** 매년
b 일 년에 열 번 쯤   **f** 며칠에 한 번
c 매일 아침   **g** 일주일에 네 번
d 이틀에 한 번   **h** 한 달에 일곱 번 쯤

SELF CHECK

	I CAN...
○	. . . list the hobbies I like and dislike.
○	. . . explain why I like or dislike an activity.
○	. . . state how frequently I do a hobby or activity.

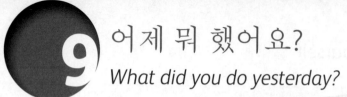

9 어제 뭐 했어요?

What did you do yesterday?

In this unit, you will learn how to:
▶ *say and describe what you did on a day in the past.*
▶ *specify when, where and with whom you did an activity.*

CEFR: *(A1) Can form simple sentences in past tense to describe activities done in the past. (A1) Can recognize and understand basic expressions to describe a day in the past.*

📷 Daily life

Koreans are well known for their diligent way of life and hardworking nature. Though official working hours are similar to the West, many 회사원 (*office workers*) voluntarily stay on to complete their 업무 (*tasks*) before the next day. Regular 회식 (*after work drinks*) are also common, allowing the 회사원 to form a bond with their 선배 (*seniors*) and 상사 (*superiors*) outside of the 회사 (*office*). Their free time to enjoy 취미 (*hobbies*) therefore tends to be quite late, meaning numerous gyms and shops are open 24 hours in Korea.

학생 (*students*) also spend long days, travelling back and forth between 학교 (*school*) and 학원 (*after-class tutoring academy*). 학생 are constantly encouraged to study long and hard as 교육 (*education*) in Korea is viewed as being crucial for success. In fact, 대한민국 (*South Korea*) tops the list of developed countries with the best education systems in the world. The 예의 (*respect*) embedded in students towards their 선생님 (*teacher*) is certainly a key factor to the system's success.

All 학생 strive to go to a good 대학교 (*university*) to give them a head start in life. Three of Korea's most prestigious 대학교 are grouped under the acronym SKY: 서울대학교 (*Seoul National University*), 고려대학교 (*Korea University*) and 연세대학교 (*Yonsei University*).

How many places of work or study are mentioned in the text? Which are part of your daily life or routine?

Vocabulary builder

09.01 **Read the vocabulary and try to pronounce each word. Then listen and try to imitate the speakers.**

DAILY LIFE

일어났어요, 잤어요	I woke up, I went to sleep
아침/점심 / 저녁 먹었어요	I ate breakfast/lunch/dinner
학교/회사 갔어요	I went to school/the office
출근했어요, 퇴근했어요	I went to work, I left work
공부했어요, 일했어요	I studied, I worked
청소했어요, 빨래했어요	I cleaned, I did the laundry
운동했어요, 요리했어요	I did sports, I cooked
골프 쳤어요, 등산했어요	I played golf, I went hiking
책 읽었어요, 그림 그렸어요	I read books, I drew pictures
음악 들었어요, 사진 찍었어요	I listened to music, I took photos
친구 만났어요, 집에 있었어요	I met a friend, I stayed at home
바빴어요, 한가했어요	I was busy, I was free
재미있었어요, 재미없었어요	it was fun, it wasn't fun
신났어요, 힘들었어요	it was exciting, it was tiring

NEW EXPRESSIONS

... 뭐 했어요?	What did you do . . . ?
언제 / 어디서 / 누구랑 . . . ?	When/Where/With who . . . ?
(장소) 에서 . . . (시간) 에 . . .	at (location/place) . . . at (time) . . .
(사람) 와/과 함께, 혼자서 . . .	. . . with (person), on my own
오늘, 어제, 그저께	today, yesterday, day before yesterday
아침, 점심, 저녁	morning, lunchtime, evening
오전, 오후	morning (a.m.), afternoon (p.m.)
낮, 밤	daytime, night
지난주, 지난 주말	last week, last weekend
그래서	and so
그 다음에, 그 전에	afterwards, before that

 Conversations

09.02 *Minsu and Cholmin are talking about what they did yesterday.*
Listen and answer the questions.

1 Did either Minsu or Cholmin play football yesterday?

민수	철민씨 어제 뭐 했어요?
철민	어제 운동했어요.
민수	누구랑 운동했어요?
철민	중기와 함께 오후에 등산했어요. 재미있었어요!
	민수씨는 어제 뭐 했어요?
민수	저는 오전에 집에 있었어요. 청소했어요. 그리고
	빨래했어요. 정말 힘들었어요.
철민	오후에는 뭐 했어요?
민수	여동생 민지랑 점심 먹었어요. 그 다음에 음악
	들었어요. 오후에는 한가했어요.

2 Read or listen to the conversation again and answer these questions.
   a What did Cholmin do yesterday? Who was he with?
   b What did Minsu do in the morning yesterday? How did he find it?
   c Who did Minsu have lunch with?
   d Was Minsu busy in the afternoon yesterday? What did he do after lunch?

3 Can you say the following in Korean?
   a What did you do the day before yesterday?
   b Where did you do sports? When did you do sports?
   c In the morning I went to work. I went to the office.
   d What did you do at night?
   e Afterwards I met a friend. I was busy.

 4 09.03 **Minsu wants to ask you about your day yesterday.**
   Continue the conversation. Use the English prompts to help you.

<u>09.04</u> *Minsu and Cholmin are discussing what they did in the morning, describing their daily routine. Listen and answer the questions.*

5 Who woke up earlier this morning, Minsu or Cholmin?

민수	오늘 아침에 뭐 했어요? 언제 일어났어요?
철민	아침 일곱시에 일어났어요. 그리고 학교 갔어요. 학교에서 공부했어요. 책도 읽었어요. 민수씨는 언제 일어났어요?
민수	저는 아홉시에 일어났어요. 그리고 오전에 친구 만났어요.
철민	어디서 만났어요?
민수	안나를 백화점에서 만났어요. 안나와 함께 점심을 먹었어요.
철민	오후에는 뭐 했어요?
민수	오후에는 한가했어요. 집에 있었어요. 집에서 그림 그렸어요. 철민씨는 오후에도 학교 갔어요?
철민	아니요. 오후에는 골프 쳤어요.
민수	누구랑 쳤어요?
철민	형이랑 골프 쳤어요.

6 Read or listen to the conversation again and answer these questions.

a What did Cholmin do in the morning after he woke up?
b What time did Minsu wake up? What did Minsu do in the morning?
c Who did Minsu have lunch with? Where did they meet?
d Was Minsu busy in the afternoon? What did he do?
e Who did Cholmin play golf with in the afternoon?

7 Can you translate the following into English?

a 아침 일곱시에 일어났어요.
b 학교에서 공부했어요. 책도 읽었어요.
c 안나와 함께 점심을 먹었어요.
d 집에 있었어요. 집에서 그림 그렸어요.
e 오후에는 골프 쳤어요.

8 <u>09.05</u> **Minsu wants to ask you about your day today. Continue the conversation. Use the English prompts to help you.**

Language discovery

Find the past tense expressions for the following in the first conversation. Can you figure out the verb ending used to form the past tense?

  a 운동해요
  b 집에 있어요

  c 점심 먹어요
  d 음악 들어요

1 PRESENT TENSE ENDINGS: -아/어/여요

So far you have learned to use the present tense with the polite ending -요. The dictionary form of verbs ends in -다. How do you form the present tense if you begin with the dictionary form? Remember: the verb stem is the dictionary form with -다 removed (see Unit 1). -아/어/여요 is attached to this 'base' form to describe the present tense. The exact verb ending depends on the vowel of the final syllable in the verb stem.

▶ If the vowel of the final syllable in the verb stem is either ㅏ or ㅗ, -아요 is used. For example, 앉다 (to sit) has verb stem 앉-. The final vowel is ㅏ, and therefore the ending -아요 is used to describe the present tense. This gives 앉아요 (I sit).

▶ If the vowel of the final syllable in the verb stem is any vowel other than ㅏ and ㅗ, the ending -어요 is used. For example, 먹다 (to eat) has verb stem 먹-. The final vowel is ㅓ, and therefore -어요 is used. This gives 먹어요 (I eat).

In either of the above two cases, if the vowel is repeated in the present tense ending, it is omitted. For example, I go is 가요 instead of 가아요, whilst I stand is also 서요 instead of 서어요. Vowels can also be combined into a complex vowel as with to see. Instead of 보아요, the ㅗ and ㅏ combine to give 봐요 (I see).

Finally, Korean has many verbs that end in -하다. Even though the vowel in the final syllable of the verb stem is ㅏ, these verbs take the verb ending -여요, not -아요. This gives -하여요 to describe the present tense, which is contracted into 해요 in everyday use. For example, 운동하다 (to do sports) ends in -하다 so the ending -여요 is added to stem 운동하-, giving 운동하여요, which is contracted to 운동해요 (I do sports) in everyday use.

2 PAST TENSE ENDINGS: -았/었/였어요

The verb endings -았/었/였어요 describe the past tense. The exact verb ending, as with the present tense above, depends on the final vowel of the verb stem.

▶ If the vowel of the final syllable in the verb stem is either ㅏ or ㅗ, the ending -았어요 is used. For example, 앉아요 (*I sit*) with final vowel ㅏ in its stem 앉- uses the past tense ending -았어요 to give 앉았어요 (*I sat*).

▶ If the vowel of the final syllable in the verb stem is any vowel other than ㅏ or ㅗ, the ending -었어요 is used. For example, 먹어요 (*I eat*) with final vowel ㅓ, neither ㅏ nor ㅗ, in its stem 먹- uses the ending -었어요 to give 먹었어요 (*I ate*).

As with present tense endings, if the vowel is repeated in the verb ending, it is omitted. For example *I went* becomes 갔어요 instead of 가았어요, while *I stood* is 섰어요 instead of 서었어요. Vowels can also be combined into a complex vowel as with *to see*. Instead of 보았어요, the ㅗ and ㅏ combine to give 봤어요 (*I saw*).

▶ Finally, for verbs ending in -하다, the past tense ending -였어요 is used. This gives verbs ending in -하였어요 to describe the past tense, which is contracted to -했어요 in everyday use. For example, 운동해요 (*I do sports*) becomes 운동하였어요 in the past tense, which is contracted to 운동했어요 (*I did sports*).

Find the particles that complete the missing blanks in the second conversation then complete the sentences. Both mean *at*, but when is each particle used?

a 아침 일곱시 _____ 일어났어요. 그리고 학교 갔어요. 학교 _____ 공부했어요.

b 저는 아홉시 _____ 일어났어요. 그리고 오전 _____ 친구 만났어요.

c 집 _____ 그림 그렸어요. 철민씨는 오후 _____ 도 학교 갔어요?

3 SAYING WHEN AND WHERE: -에 , -에서

Both particles -에 and -에서 translate as *at* in English. However -에 is used after a noun indicating the time, whereas -에서 is used after a noun indicating the place or location something was done. For example, the sentence *I ate lunch at home at 1 o'clock* becomes 1시에 집에서 점심 먹었어요.

Practice

1 Complete the sentences with the correct particle for *at*.

a 지난 주말 영화관 _____ 친구 만났어요. 낮 _____ 친구와 함께 점심 먹었어요.

b 어제 아침 _____ 출근했어요. 그리고 회사 _____ 일했어요. 저녁 여덟시 _____ 퇴근했어요. 너무 바빴어요.

c 지난 주 월요일 오전 _____ 집 _____ 청소했어요. 오후_____ 는 빨래했어요.

d 오늘 오전 열시 _____ 일어났어요. 식당 _____ 아침 먹었어요.

2 Look at the list of English verb phrases with Korean verb stems. Give the correct verb ending then the complete phrase. Consider any omissions and contractions.

Example: I play football: 축구하-   -여요   축구해요

a I study: 공부하-   **i** I studied: 공부하-

b I play: 놀-   **j** I played: 놀-

c I wake up: 일어나-   **k** I woke up: 일어나-

d I meet: 만나-   **l** I met: 만나-

e I go hiking: 등산하-   **m** I went hiking: 등산하-

f I stand: 서-   **n** I stood: 서-

g I see: 보-   **o** I saw: 보-

h I cook: 요리하-   **p** I cooked: 요리하-

3 <u>09.06</u> **Say the following out loud then listen and check your answers.**

a Say you went to work this morning at 7 o'clock.

b Say you met a friend at a restaurant in the afternoon. Say you ate dinner with Jane and that it was fun.

c Say you listened to music at school. Say you also read books afterwards.

d Say you played golf with Ben last week. Say it was tiring.

e Say you studied on your own at home yesterday. Say you did the laundry afterwards and ate dinner at 6 o'clock. Say you were very busy.

f Say you left work at 10 o'clock in the evening the day before yesterday.

Speaking

Peter is asking you what you did last weekend. Answer his questions and ask him about his weekend, too.

Peter	지난 주말에 뭐 했어요?
You	*Say on the Saturday you were free. Say you were at home and you cleaned.*
Peter	그럼 일요일에는 뭐 했어요?
You	*Say you met a friend on Sunday. Say you ate lunch with Susan at a restaurant.*
Peter	그 다음에 뭐 했어요?
You	*Say you played golf afterwards at 3 o'clock in the afternoon. Say it was very fun. Then ask Peter what he did last weekend.*
Peter	저는 바빴어요. 토요일 아침에 출근했어요. 그리고 일요일에는 친구와 함께 등산했어요.
You	*Ask Peter when he left work on Saturday.*
Peter	저녁 여덟시에 퇴근했어요. 그리고 집에서 요리했어요.

Listening

1 <u>09.07</u> **Listen to Thomas and Sarah's conversation. Then read the statements and answer true or false.**

   a Sarah woke up at 6 o'clock yesterday morning.
   b Sarah ate breakfast at half past seven in the morning.
   c Sarah went to work at 8 o'clock and left at seven in the evening.
   d Thomas played badminton in the morning with a friend called Ben.
   e Thomas played football in the afternoon with his two brothers.
   f Thomas said football was very exciting, but really tiring.

2 <u>09.08</u> **Listen to this conversation between Jongmin and Taesu and answer the questions that follow.**

   a What did Taesu do at home yesterday? Was he on his own?
   b What did Jongmin do with his friend yesterday? How did he find it?
   c What did Jongmin do with his older brother yesterday? How did he find it?

Reading and writing

1 Read the email from Jongmin below and answer the questions.

안녕하세요! 토마스씨는 지난 주에 뭐 했어요?바빴어요? 저는 정말
바빴어요. 월요일과 화요일에는회사 갔어요. 아침 일곱시에 출근했어요.
그리고 저녁 여덟시 쯤에 퇴근했어요. 너무 힘들었어요. 점심과 저녁을
회사에서 먹었어요. 토마스씨도 일했어요?언제 퇴근했어요?

수요일에는 운동했어요. 오전에는 누나와 함께 탁구 쳤어요. 그리고
오후에는 혼자서 등산했어요. 토마스씨도 지난 주에 운동했어요? 목
요일에는 집에 있었어요. 혼자서 청소했어요. 그리고 집에서 요리도
했어요. 재미있었어요!

그리고 금요일에는 친구 만났어요. 친구와 함께 식당에서 점심 먹었어
요. 그리고 백화점에서 사진 찍었어요.

a How does Jongmin describe his past week – was he busy or free?
b On which days did he go to work? What time did he go to and leave
   work? Where did he eat his lunch and dinner during these days?
c Which sports did Jongmin do on Wednesday and with whom did he
   play?
d Did Jongmin stay at home on Thursday? What did he do?
e What day did Jongmin meet his friend? What did they do together?

**2 Thomas is having trouble understanding the Korean email.
Translate it for him into English.**

**3 Now reply to Jongmin's email as Thomas. Address the email
to Jongmin, put it in Korean and don't forget to answer all the
questions Jongmin asks.**

Test yourself

1 How would you do the following?

  a Ask what someone did in the night on the day before yesterday.

  _____

  b Say you drew pictures at school. Say it was fun.

  _____

  c Say you stayed at home and cooked on your own at home.

  _____

  d Ask someone when they went to sleep yesterday night.

  _____

  e Say you went to work with your friend at 8 o'clock in the morning.

  _____

2 Match the particles and definitions.

  a -에서   **1** meaning *at*, used after a location or place

  b -와/과 함께   **2** meaning *at*, used after a time

  c -에   **3** meaning *with*, used after a person

3 Give the correct verb ending for the following. Use the given verb stems to determine the exact ending.

  a I received: 받-   **e** I sing: 노래하-

  b I greet: 인사하-   **f** I sat: 앉-

  c I pushed: 밀-   **g** I eat: 먹-

  d I read (present); 읽-   **h** I read (past); 읽-

SELF CHECK

I CAN...
... list and comment on activities done in the past.
... state when, where and with whom I did an activity.

10 주말에 뭐 할 거예요?

What will you do at the weekend?

In this unit, you will learn how to:
▶ *say what you will do in the future.*
▶ *make a suggestion about what to do in the future.*
▶ *make an appointment to meet in the future.*

CEFR: *(A1) Can form simple sentences using the future tense to describe activities that will be done in the future. (A1) Can recognize and understand basic expressions to make an appointment to meet in the future.*

 Weekends

The 주말 (*weekend*) is a time for family activities and catching up with 친구 (*friends*). Koreans lead such busy lives that they often only have time to completely relax and socialize during the 주말. 부모님 (*parents*) get a break from 회사 (*office*) while the children get away from their busy weekly schedules of 학교 (*school*) and 학원 (*after-school tutoring academy*). Many families make the most of the 주말 by going out for a family 식사 (*meal*) or even 당일치기 여행 (*day trips*) to 도시 (*cities*) outside the 수도 (*capital*), 서울 (*Seoul*). The well-established high speed rail system KTX – Korea Train eXpress – makes this ever more possible with its 305 km/h 기차 (*trains*).

Making appointments to meet

When Korean friends meet up, they don't always decide what to do beforehand. Instead, it is more common to decide a 시간 (*time*) and 장소 (*location*) first then decide what to do once together. Popular places to meet include 강남 (*Gangnam*), 압구정 (*Apgujeong*) and 이태원 (*Itaewon*).

Do you know which popular meeting place mentioned in the text is also the setting of South Korean star Psy's global hit single '강남 Style'?

Vocabulary builder

10.01 **Read the vocabulary and try to pronounce each word. Then listen and try to imitate the speakers.**

WEEKEND ACTIVITIES

쇼핑해요.	I go shopping.
극장에서 연극 봐요.	I watch a play at the theatre.
영화 봐요.	I watch a film.
박물관 / 미술관 . . . 가요.	I go to . . . the museum/gallery.
커피숍 가요.	I go to a coffee shop.
축구 경기 보러 가요.	I go to watch a football match.
놀이공원에 놀러 가요.	I go to a theme park.
목욕탕 가요.	I go to the public baths.

NEW EXPRESSIONS

. . . 에 시간 있어요?	Do you have time on . . . ?
시간 있어요 / 시간 없어요.	I do have time/I don't have time.
일이 있어요.	I have something to do.
(이미) 약속이 있어요.	I (already) have an appointment.
. . . 에 만날까요?	Shall we meet on . . . ?
. . . 에서 만나요!	Let's meet at . . . !
어때요?	How does it sound?
좋아요!/안 돼요.	Sounds good!/I can't do that.
. . . 에 뭐 할 거예요?	What will you do on . . . ?
집에 있을 거예요.	I will stay at home.
친구 만날 거예요.	I will meet a friend.
. . . 갈 거예요.	I will go to . . .
다음주 (주말)	next week (weekend)
내일, 모레	tomorrow, day after tomorrow
그때 봐요!	See you then!
다음에 봐요 그럼.	See you another time then.

 Conversations

10.02 *Haeri is asking Yongsu about their plans for the upcoming weekend. Listen and answer the questions.*

1 Does Yongsu have plans for the whole weekend?

해리	용수씨, 주말에 뭐 할 거예요?
용수	토요일에 약속 있어요. 친구 만날 거예요.
해리	어디서 만날 거예요?
용수	강남 역 삼 번 출구 앞에서 만날 거예요.
해리	일요일에는 뭐 할 거예요?
용수	일요일에는 약속 없어요. 한가해요.
해리	그럼 일요일에 만날까요?
용수	네! 좋아요! 일요일에 만나요!
해리	두시에 백화점 앞에서 만나요! 그때 봐요!

2 Read or listen to the conversation again and answer these questions.

a Where is Yongsu meeting his friend on Saturday?

b What is Yongsu doing on Sunday?

c What day does Haeri suggest they meet up?

d At what time and where do Haeri and Yongsu agree to meet?

3 Say the following in Korean.

a What will you do on Tuesday?

b I don't have time on Saturday.

c I will meet him in front of the school.

d I have an appointment on Sunday. I am busy.

e Let's meet at 7p.m. in front of the restaurant.

 4 10.03 **Haeri wants to ask you about your plans for the weekend. What are you going to do? Continue the conversation. Use the English prompts to help you.**

5 What day are Jisu and Dana meeting up?

지수	다음주 언제 만날까요?
다나	목요일에는 일 있어요. 학교 갈 거예요. 수요일에 만날까요?
지수	좋아요. 시간 있어요. 수요일에 만나요! 신촌 역에서 만날까요?
다나	아니요 버스 정류장에서 만나요! 수요일에 뭐 할까요?
지수	저는 축구를 좋아해요. 축구 경기 보러 가요! 어때요?
다나	안 돼요. 저는 축구 싫어해요. 영화 좋아해요?
지수	네 영화 보는 것 좋아해요. 영화 볼까요?
다나	네 영화 봐요! 그리고 저녁에는 커피숍 가요!
지수	좋아요! 언제 만날까요?
다나	네시 반에 만나요. 버스 정류장에서!
지수	그때 봐요! 안녕히 가세요!

6 Read or listen to the conversation again and answer these questions.

   a Why can't Dana meet on the Thursday? Where will she be going that day?

   b Where does Jisu suggest they meet? Where does Dana suggest?

   c What does Jisu suggest they do on Wednesday? What does Dana think about it?

   d What do Jisu and Dana eventually agree to do?

   e Where does Dana suggest they go in the evening?

   f What time will they meet?

7 Translate the following into English.

   a 다음주 언제 만날까요?

   b 좋아요. 시간 있어요. 수요일에 만나요!

   c 수요일에 뭐 할까요?

   d 축구 경기 보러 가요! 어때요?

   e 네 영화 보는 것 좋아해요. 영화 볼까요?

   f 그때 봐요! 안녕히 가세요!

Language discovery

 Find the sentences in the conversations. What endings are used to form the future tense and make suggestions?

   a What will you do at the weekend?

   b I will meet a friend.

   c Then shall we meet on Sunday?

   d Shall we watch a film?

1 FUTURE TENSE ENDINGS: -(으)ㄹ 거예요

The ending -(으)ㄹ 거예요 indicates a future plan or intention and translates as *will* or *going to do something*. This ending takes two forms depending on the last letter of the verb stem.

▶ If the stem ends in a vowel or the consonant ㄹ, the ending -ㄹ 거예요 is used. For example the verb 만나다 (*to meet*) has stem 만나- which ends with the vowel ㅏ. Similarly the verb 놀다 (*to play*) has stem 놀- ending with the consonant ㄹ. Both therefore use -ㄹ 거예요 to form the future tense. This gives 만날 거예요 (*I will meet*) and 놀 거예요 (*I will play*).

▶ If the stem ends in a consonant other than ㄹ, the ending -을 거예요 is used. For example the verb 먹다 (*to eat*) has stem 먹-. This therefore uses the ending -을 거예요 to give 먹을 거예요 (*I will eat*) to form the future tense.

2 MAKING SUGGESTIONS: -(으)ㄹ 까요?

As you will remember from Unit 5, -(으)ㄹ 까요? is used when making a suggestion or asking someone about his/her preference, and translates into *Shall I . . . ?* or *Shall we . . . ?* As with other verb endings, the exact form depends on the last letter of the verb stem.

▶ If the verb stem ends in a vowel or the consonant ㄹ, the ending -ㄹ까요? is used, whilst -을까요? is used for stems ending in any consonant other than ㄹ. For example, 만날까요? (*Shall we meet?*), 놀까요? (*Shall we play?*) and 먹을까요? (*Shall we eat?*).

Find these sentences in the second conversation. Which new sentence structure is being introduced?

　a　Let's meet on Wednesday!

　b　Let's go (to) watch a football match!

　c　Let's watch a film!

3 MAKING A PROPOSITION

Take the expression 영화 봐요. In the Vocabulary builder this has been introduced as meaning *I watch a film*. However in the conversations the phrase 영화 봐요! has been translated and understood as the proposition *Let's watch a film!* The only notable difference is the addition of an exclamation mark. Does this mean all sentences become a proposition with an exclamation mark? Well, not necessarily.

The polite present tense verb ending -아/어/여요 can be used for all four sentence types (statement, command, propositive and question) depending on the context and intonation. That is, the single expression 읽어요 can mean *I read* (statement), *Read* (command), *Let's read* (propositive) or *Do you read?* (question).

In this unit the propositive form has been introduced and used extensively as suggestions are being made for future plans. Remember, though: Always check the context of the sentence to determine which sentence type the expression is describing.

4 'GO (TO) DO SOMETHING': -(으)러 가요

The ending -(으)러 가요 translates as *go to do something*. It indicates the reason as to why you are going somewhere. For example, the expression 축구 경기 보러 가요! translates into *Let's go to watch a football match!*

▶　The exact ending depends on the last letter of the verb stem. If the verb stem ends in a vowel or the consonant ㄹ, -러 가요 is used. For example, 만나러 가요 (*Let's go to meet*) and 놀러 가요 (*Let's go to play*) If the verb stem ends in a consonant other than ㄹ, -으러 가요 is used. For example, 먹으러 가요 (*Let's go to eat*).

🔓 Practice

1 **Read the statements then complete the translations with the correct verb ending for each stem.**

   a I will eat dinner with a friend: 친구와 함께 저녁 [먹-] _____.

   b Shall we meet in front of the post office?: 우체국 앞에서 [만나-] _____?

   c Let's go to watch a film at 6 p.m.: 여섯시에 영화 [보-] _____.

   d Shall we stay at home?: 집에 [있-] _____?

   e Let's eat breakfast at 8 a.m.: 여덟시에 아침 [먹-] _____.

   f I will go to the coffee shop: 커피숍에 [가-] _____.

2 **Look at each expression. Attach a correct future tense verb ending to create a statement and then translate it.**

Example: 쇼핑하-   쇼핑할 거예요. *I will go shopping.*

   a 목욕탕에 가-   **e** 배드민턴 치-

   b 우표 모으-   **f** 여행하-

   c 그림 그리-   **g** 미술관 가-

   d 놀이동산에 놀러 가-   **h** 극장에서 영화 보-

3 **Change the propositive statements into suggestive questions.**

Example: 내일 아홉시에 만나요!   내일 아홉시에 만날까요?

   a 점심 먹어요!   **e** 책 읽어요!

   b 목욕탕 가요!   **f** 등산하러 가요!

   c 다나씨랑 놀아요!   **g** 음악 들어요!

   d 여기 앉아요!   **h** 기차 타요!

4 <u>10.05</u> **Say your answers out loud then listen and check your answers.**

   a Say you will go to see a film tomorrow. Say you will go with a friend.

   b Ask Jisu what she is doing next weekend. Suggest meeting up on Saturday.

   c Suggest eating dinner at Arirang restaurant at half past seven tonight.

   d Propose going to the museum on Monday. Ask how it sounds.

   e Say you have something to do on Friday. Say you will study at school.

Speaking

Richard is asking you about your plans for the weekend. Answer his questions and ask him about his plans too.

Richard	주말에 뭐 할 거예요? 약속 있어요?
You	*Say Yes, you have an appointment. Say you are busy. Say you will meet a friend on Friday evening and will go to the museum on Saturday.*
Richard	박물관은 누구랑 갈 거예요?
You	*Say you will go to the museum with your mother.*
Richard	일요일에도 약속 있어요?
You	*Say No, you don't have plans on Sunday. Say you will be at home. Ask Richard what he will do on Sunday. Suggest meeting up for dinner.*
Richard	좋아요! 저는 한가해요. 저녁에 갈비 먹어요! 어때요?
You	*Say it sounds good and propose meeting in front of the restaurant at seven o'clock.*
Richard	네. 그때 봐요!

Listening

1 <u>10.06</u> **Listen to the following people talk about their plans for the weekend. Match the names to the plans.**

a	Nina	**1**	Will go to the office and work.
b	Bill	**2**	Will stay at home and clean. In the afternoon will play golf.
c	Katy		
d	Peter	**3**	Will meet younger brother and go watch a football match.
		4	Will go watch a football match with father and older brother.

2 <u>10.07</u> **Listen to the conversation between Minjae and Hojin and answer the questions.**

  a What day do Minjae and Hojin decide to meet? Why don't they meet tomorrow?

  b Why will they meet in the evening rather than the morning?

  c What do they agree to do when they meet up?

  d Where and at what time will they meet?

Reading and writing

1 Read the email from Kanghun and answer the questions.

로버트씨 안녕하세요! 다음주 목요일에 시간 있어요? 바빠요? 약속
없으면 만날까요? 저녁 먹으러 가요! 잠실 역 근처 식당에서 비빔밥
먹어요. 그리고 그 다음에 커피숍이나 영화관 가요! 저녁 일곱시 쯤에
만날까요? 어디서 만날까요?

저는 목요일 오전에 집에 있을 거예요. 그리고 밤에는 운동하러 갈
거예요. 그래서 저녁에만 시간 있어요. 수요일에는 회사 갈 거예요.
그리고 금요일에도 일 있어요. 친구와 함께 목욕탕 갈 거예요. 하지
만 주말에는 약속 없어요. 주말에도 집에 있을 거예요. 집에서 청소할
거예요. 그리고 음악 들을 거예요. 그럼 언제 볼까요?

a Which day does Kanghun suggest they meet?
b What does Kanghun suggest they do that day? What time does he suggest?
c What will Kanghun be doing on Thursday morning and Thursday at night?
d What are Kanghun's plans for Wednesday and Friday?
e Does Kanghun have any plans for the weekend? What will he do?

2 Robert is having trouble understanding the Korean email. Translate it for him into English.

3 Now reply to Kanghun's email as Robert. Address the email to Kanghun, write it in Korean and don't forget to answer all the questions Kanghun asks.

? Test yourself

1 How would you do the following?
  a Ask someone what s/he will do next Monday. Ask if s/he has plans.

  _____

  b Say you already have an appointment. Say you have something to do.

  _____

c Say you will go and do sports. Say you will also go to watch a football match.

_____

d Suggest meeting at 3 o'clock tomorrow afternoon in front of the school.

_____

e Propose watching a play at the theatre with Martin.

_____

f Suggest going shopping. Propose meeting behind the department store.

_____

2 Match the verb endings and descriptions.

a	-어요	**1**	making a proposition, verb stem's final vowel is ㅓ
b	-아요		
c	-여요	**2**	making a suggestion, verb stem ends with consonant ㄹ
d	-ㄹ 거예요		
e	-을 거예요	**3**	making a proposition, verb stem's final vowel is ㅏ
g	-을 까요?		
h	-러 가요	**4**	future tense, verb stem ends with vowel ㅓ
i	-으러 가요	**5**	making a suggestion, verb stem ends with consonant ㄱ

6 future tense, verb stem ends with consonant ㅂ

7 making a proposition, verb stem's final syllable is 하-

8 meaning *go to do something*, verb stem ends with vowel ㅗ

9 meaning *go to do something*, verb stem ends with consonant ㄱ

SELF CHECK

	I CAN. . .
○	. . . say what I will do in the future.
○	. . . ask someone about his/her plans for the future.
○	. . . make a suggestion about what to do in the future.
○	. . . make plans to meet up in the future.

Review

1 **Translate the sentences into English. Pay attention to how you express the underlined particles.**

a 힘들고 지루하지만 건강에 좋아요.

b 매주 운동해요. 요즘에는 일주일에 세 번 운동해요.

c 식당 앞에서 저녁 여덟시에 만나요.

d 압구정에서 강남까지 십오분 쯤 걸려요. 광화문보다 더 가까워요.

e 서울 역에서 버스 타야돼요. 버스 밖에 없어요. 거기까지 가는 지하철은 없어요.

f 버스로 가는 것이 제일 빨라요.

g 한 달에 다섯 번 등산 해요. 재미있고 스트레스가 풀려요.

2 **Match the sentences in Korean with the English translations. Look at the verb endings for clues. There are four extra English translations. What are their Korean equivalents?**

a 일요일에 영화관 가고 싶어요. 영화 보고 싶어요.

b 강남은 지하철 타고 갈 수 있어요.

c 저기서 버스 타야 돼요. 지하철은 없어요.

d 농구 하러 가요! 내일 갈까요?

e 여기서 갈아타야 돼요? 옥수에서도 갈아탈 수 있어요?

f 놀이공원에 가고 싶어요! 다음주 주말에 갈까요?

g 저녁에 만날까요? 오늘 학교 가야 돼요?

i Do I have to transfer here? Can I transfer at Oksu?

ii You can get the bus over there. There is also the subway.

iii I want to go to the cinema on Sunday. I want to watch a film.

iv Let's go play basketball! Shall we go tomorrow?

v Shall I transfer here? Do I have to transfer at Oksu?

vi Shall we meet in the evening? Do you have to go to school today?

vii You can take the subway to Gangnam.

viii Can you meet in the evening? Shall we go to school today?

ix I want to go to the theme park! Shall we go next weekend?

x You have to get the bus over there. There is no subway.

xi I want to play basketball! Shall we play now?

3 Complete the table. Note that the present, past and future tenses have been constructed from the single verb stem.

Verb stem	Present tense	Past tense	Future tense
만나-	만나요	만났어요	만날 거예요.
가-	가요	a _____	b _____
먹-	c _____	먹었어요	d _____
그리-	그려요	e _____	f _____
하-	해요	했어요	할 거예요
놀-	g _____	h _____	놀 거예요.
마시-	마셔요	i _____	j _____
보-	k _____	봤어요	l _____
좋아하-	m _____	n _____	좋아할 거예요
앉-	o _____	앉았어요	p _____
입-	q _____	입었어요	r _____
말하-	말해요	s _____	t _____
주-	줘요	u _____	v _____
읽-	w _____	x _____	읽을 거예요
섞-	y _____	섞었어요	z _____

4 Bongsoon and Wansoo are talking about what they like to do in their free time and what they did last weekend. Read their conversation then answer the questions that follow.

봉순	완수씨는 취미가 뭐예요? 운동 좋아해요?
완수	네 운동 정말 좋아해요!
봉순	무슨 운동을 좋아해요? 저는 야구 좋아해요!
완수	저도 야구 정말 좋아해요! 그리고 축구와 배드민턴도 좋아해요. 축구는 거의 매일 하고 배드민턴은 요즘 일주일에 두 번 쳐요.
봉순	축구를 왜 좋아해요? 축구는 너무 힘들고 어려워요.
완수	힘들지만 재미있고 건강에 좋아요! 그럼 봉선씨는 왜 야구 좋아해요?
봉순	야구는 신나요! 그리고 스트레스가 풀려요!
완수	야구 자주 해요?
봉순	아니요 저는 야구 보는 것을 좋아해요. 그래서 야구 보러 자주 가요.
완수	얼마나 자주 가요? 한 달에 한번?
봉순	아니요! 거의 매주 가요!
완수	지난주 주말에도 야구 보러 갔어요?
봉순	네! 토요일 오후에 야구 경기 봤어요. 그리고 저녁에는 친구 만났어요.
완수	일요일에는 뭐 했어요?
봉순	집에 있었어요. 청소했어요. 완수씨는 지난주 주말에 뭐 했어요?
완수	저도 일요일에는 집에 있었어요. 그리고 토요일에는 친구 다섯명과 함께 축구 했어요. 오전에 축구하고 저녁에는 함께 밥 먹었어요.

a Does Wansoo like sports? Which sports does he like other than badminton?

b How often does Wansoo play badminton? Which sport does he play nearly every day?

c What does Bongsoon think of football? What does Wansoo think of football?

d Why does Bongsoon like baseball? Does she play often?

e How often does she go and watch a baseball match? Did she go last weekend?

f Give as many details as possible about what Bongsoon did on Saturday.

g Did Bongsoon go out on Sunday? What did Wansoo do on Sunday?

h List everything Wansoo did last Saturday. How many friends was he with?

5 Dongju and Jimin are deciding on a time and place to meet up next week. Dongju is new to the area so Jimin gives him directions to the meeting place. Read their conversation then answer the questions that follow.

동주	지민씨 다음주에 시간 있어요? 만날까요?
지민	시간 있어요. 네, 만나요!
동주	언제 만날래요? 그리고 뭐 하고 싶어요?
지민	월요일부터 목요일까지는 출근해야 돼요. 그리고 금요일에는 약속이 있어요. 토요일 어때요?
동주	안돼요. 토요일에 약속 있어요.
지민	그럼 일요일!
동주	네 좋아요. 일요일에 봐요! 저 영화 보고 싶어요. 영화 보러 갈까요?
지민	영화 보고 저녁도 먹어요! 영화관 근처에 식당 있어요. 아리랑 식당. 정말 맛있어요!
동주	좋아요! 몇 시에 볼까요?
지민	영화관 앞에서 네 시에 만나요! 어때요?
동주	영화관이 어디에 있어요?
지민	압구정 역 근처예요. 압구정 역에서 오 분 밖에 안걸려요.
동주	압구정 역까지는 어떻게 가요?
지민	지하철로 가면 삼 호선을 타야 돼요. 버스도 탈 수 있지만 많이 느려요. 지하철이 제일 빨라요.
동주	버스는 몇 번 버스를 타야 돼요? 갈아타야 돼요?
지민	사백오십육번 버스나 사백이십번 버스 타세요. 그리고 압구정 역에서 내리세요. 사십분 쯤 걸려요.
동주	네! 고마워요. 그럼 일요일 오후 4시, 영화관 앞에서 봐요!
지민	네! 그때 봐요!

a Why isn't Jimin free during the week? Are there any days Dongju can't meet up?

b Which day do they decide to meet?

c What does Dongju want to do? What is the final plan for the entire day?

d Where and at what time will they meet? How far away is their meeting point from Apgujeong station?

e Which line on the subway must Dongju take to Apgujeong?

f Can Dongju take any buses? How long does it take to get to Apgujeong by bus?

g Which is the route Jimin recommends?

Answer key

Greeting, bowing and names

You would expect to be greeted with the expression 안녕하세요 and addressed with the polite title -씨 after your name, whether they use just your first name or your full name. For example, 안녕하세요 민우씨 or 안녕하세요 최민우씨.

Conversations

1 The first student is called 이철수. The second student is called 김상민.
2 The lady's name is 최한별.
3 a Korean, **b** Doctor
4 a 안녕하세요. 저는 최한별이에요. **b** 저는 한국 사람이에요. **c** 저는 의사예요. **d** 만나서 반가워요.
5 No, the two don't seem to have met before. They do not know each other as they are introducing themselves to one another. They also use the phrase 만나서 반가워요 (*Nice to meet you*), suggesting they have met for the first time.
6 a American, **b** Teacher
7 a 저는 지미 스미스예요. **b** 어느 나라 사람이에요? **c** 저는 미국 사람이에요. **d** 직업이 뭐예요? **e** 저는 선생이에요.
8 a 예요, 반가워요, **b** 어느, 나라, **c** 사람, **d** 직업, **e** 이에요

Language discovery

a 저는 선생이에요. **b** 저는 미국 사람이에요.; The Korean for *I am . . .* is 저는.

Practice

1 a 1, **b** 3, **c** 4, **d** 2
2 a 사라씨, 어느 나라 사람이에요? **b** 매튜씨, 직업이 뭐예요? **c** 저는 영국 사람이에요. **d** 저는 선생이에요. **e** Q: 지민씨, 어느 나라 사람이에요? A: 저는 한국 사람이에요. **f** Q: 영민씨, 직업이 뭐예요? A: 저는 의사예요.
3 a 이에요, **b** 이에요, **c** 이에요, **d** 예요, **e** 이에요, **f** 예요, **g** 예요

Speaking

Greeting: 안녕하세요.; 저는 … (name) … 이에요/예요. 만나서 반가워요.; 저는 … (occupation) … 이에요/예요. 지민씨 직업이 뭐예요?; 어느 나라 사람이에요? 저는 … (nationality) … 이에요.; see you: 다음에 또 봐요. 안녕히 가세요.

Listening

1 a 1 Tom, **2** British, **3** Office worker, **b 1** Suzy, **2** Chinese, **3** Housewife
2 a Fiona, **b** Australian, **c** Teacher

Reading and writing

1 a 김동수 Dongsoo Kim, **b** 요리사 Chef
2 a Amy, **b** British, **c** teacher
3 에이미씨, 안녕하세요! 만나서 반가워요! 저는 마이클이에요. 저는 영국 사람이에요. 저는 요리사예요.
4 에이미씨, 안녕하세요! 만나서 반가워요! 저는 (name)이에요/예요. 저는 (nationality)이에요. 저는 (occupation)이에요/예요.

Test yourself

1 a 안녕하세요. 만나서 반가워요. **b** 안녕히 가세요. 다음에 또 봐요. **c** 저는 (name) 이에요/예요. **d** 저는 (nationality)이에요. **e** 저는 (occupation)이에요/예요. **f** 어느 나라 사람이에요? **g** 직업이 뭐예요?
2 a 이에요, **b** 이에요, **c** 이에요, **d** 예요, **e** 이에요, **f** 예요

UNIT 2

Family values and traditions

우리 means *our* in Korean and is used as *my* when talking about or introducing family members. If 아내 means *wife*, *my wife* would become 우리 아내.

Conversations

1 No. Yongho does not live with any grandparents.
2 a 4 people. Yongho, his father, his mother and his younger sister. **b** 최민관 Minkwan Choi. He is a professor and 42 years old. **c** Yongmi is Yongho's younger sister. She is 13 years old.
3 a There are four people in my family. **b** My father, mother, younger sister and me. **c** What is your father's name? **d** My father is a professor. **e** And/Also how old is he/she? **f** Yongmi is 13 years old.
4 Sample answer: 우리 가족은 … 명이에요. 우리 … (list family members) … 하고 저예요.

우리 ... (family member) ... 이에요/예요.
... (name) ... 이에요/예요/이세요/세요.
우리 ... (family member) ... 은/는 ... (occupation) ... 이에요/예요/
이세요/세요.
5 최수빈 Subin Choi.
6 a Subin is Jangho's wife. **b** Minjun is a professor. He is 35 years old.
c Yes he is married. He has two children – a son and a daughter.
7 a 인사해요. 우리 남동생이에요. **b** 민준씨는 변호사예요. 그리고
스물아홉살이에요. **c** 아이 세명 있어요.
8 a 3, **b** 4, **c** 5, **d** 1, **e** 2

Language discovery

The common syllable -는 is the topic particle, pointing out the topic of
the sentence – the thing that is being talked about. The sentence endings
also vary between -이에요, -예요, -이세요 and -세요. These are the
normal and honorific (polite variation used to respect social elders) verb
endings which vary depending on the preceding noun's final letter.

Practice

1 a 서른여섯 서른여섯살 (no change), **b** 여든넷; 여든네살 (넷 loses
its final letter ㅅ), **c** 열아홉; 열아홉살 (no change), **d** 일흔다섯;
일흔다섯살 (no change), **e** 예순여덟; 예순여덟살 (no change),
f 마흔하나; 마흔한살 (하나 loses its final letter ㅏ), **g** 스물셋; 스물세살
(셋 loses its final letter ㅅ), **h** 쉰둘; 쉰두살 (둘 loses its final letter ㄹ)
2 a 은, 이에요, **b** 는, 이세요, **c** 은, 세요, **d** 은, 이에요, **e** 은, 이에요,
f 는, 이에요, **g** 은, 이에요, **h** 은, 예요
3 a 준수씨, 할아버지는 연세가 어떻게 되세요? **b** 용호씨, 어머니는
성함이 어떻게 되세요? **c** 우리 아버지는 쉰두살이세요. **d** 우리
여동생은 주부예요. **e** Q: 제임스씨 딸은 나이가 몇살이에요? A: 우리
딸은 일곱살이에요. **f** Q: 제임스씨 아들은 이름이 뭐예요? A: 우리
아들은 매튜예요.

Speaking

Your family: 우리 가족은 다섯명이에요. 우리 아버지, 어머니, 형,
여동생하고 저예요. **Father's age:** 우리 아버지는 예순한살이세요.
Mother's job: 우리 어머니는 회사원이세요. **Brother:** 우리 형은
서른세살이에요. 예, 결혼 했어요. 딸 있어요. **Younger sister:** 우리
여동생은 준희예요. 그리고 스물다섯살. 이에요.

Listening

1 a 2, **b** 3, **c** 1
2 a F; **b** F; **c** T; **d** F; **e** T; **f** F

Reading and writing

1 a 6 people, **b** The father is a lawyer and the mother is a civil servant. **c** 2 children: a daughter and son, **d** Male. He calls his older sister 누나 **nuna**, indicating he is male. **e** Youngest child. His other sibling is an older sister. **f** Student

2 a 55 years old, **b** Professor, **c** Mary, **d** Wife, **e** Housewife, **f** Michael, **g** 30 years old, **h** Lawyer, **i** Jennifer, **j** Daughter, **k** 27 years old

3 Refer to passage in question 2 for model answer.

Test yourself

1 a 우리 가족은 . . . (number) . . . 명이에요. **b** 우리 아버지/어머니는 . . . (occupation) . . . 이세요/세요. . . . (age) . . . 살이세요. **c** 우리 . . . (sibling relationship) . . . 은/는 . . . (name) . . . 이에요/예요. . . . (age) . . . 살이에요. 그리고 . . . (occupation) . . . 이에요. **d** 58 쉰여덟, 92 아흔둘, 17 열일곱, 34 서른넷

2 a 6, **b** 3, **c** 4, **d** 5, **e** 1, **f** 2

3 a 는 세요. **b** 은 이에요. **c** 는 이세요. **d** 는 이에요.

UNIT 3

The calendar, The climate

설날 in the West is known as the Lunar New Year, or the Chinese New Year. 추석 is similar to the American Thanksgiving.

Conversations

1 No. It isn't the weekend.

2 a 22nd August, **b** Tuesday, **c** 2.34 p.m. **d** Juri says the weather is good! It is warm and clear.

3 a 요일, **b** 무슨 요일이에요?, **c** 오후, **d** 몇 시예요?, **e** 날씨, **f** 날씨가 어때요?, **g** 그리고, **h** 맑아요

4 Sample answer: 오늘 . . . (month) . . . 월 . . . (day) . . . 일이에요.; . . . (day of the week) . . . 이에요.
지금 . . . (hour) . . . 시 . . . (minute) . . . 분이에요.; 오늘 . . . (describe the weather) . . .

5 Sangsu is older.

6 a Juri's birthday is 5th April. She was born in 1991. **b** Sangsu's birthday is 21st February. He was born in 1987. **c** Sangsu is 26 years old. **d** Juri is 22 years old. Sangsu is older.

7 u 제 생일은 구월 삼십일이에요. **b** 저는 천구백구십년생이에요. **c** 저는 스물아홉살이에요.

8 a 무슨 요일이에요? **b** 지금 몇시예요 **c** 오늘 몇월 며칠이에요?
d 생일이 언제예요? **e** 몇년생이에요? **f** 몇살이에요?

Language discovery

The particles -이 and -가 represent the subject particle. They follow the
nouns of the sentence that are doing the action/verb. In this case the
subject of the sentence is what is being described.

Practice

1 a 오전 열시 구분, **b** 천구백팔십이년 사월 이십구일, **c** 저녁 열한시
십오분전, **d** 오후/저녁 일곱시 이십오분, **e** 이천일년 시월 십오일,
f 오후 다섯시 오십오분, **g** 십이월 삼십일일 목요일, **h** 유월 십육일
일요일
2 a 가, **b** 이, **c** 가, **d** 이, **e** 이, **f** 이, **g** 가
3 a Q: 마틴씨 생일이 언제예요? 그리고 몇살이에요? A:제 생일은
유월 십이일이에요. 그리고 저는 서른한살이에요. **b** Q: 사라씨
몇년생이에요? A: 저는 천구백칠십육년생이에요. **c** 오늘 무슨
요일이에요? **d** 지금 몇시예요? **e** 오늘 날씨가 나빠요. 바람이
불어요. 그리고 추워요. **f** 오늘 맑아요. 그리고 더워요.

Speaking

Birthdays: 제 생일은 시월 이십오일이에요. 수진씨 생일이
언제예요? **Birth year:** 저는 천구백팔십구년생이에요. **Sumin:** 수민씨
생일이 언제예요? **Sujin:** 수진씨는 몇년생이에요?

Listening

1 a 수요일, 일곱; 7 a.m. Wednesday, **b** 삼십일, 반; half past 3 in the
afternoon (3.30 p.m.) 31st December, **c** 오, 오, 아홉, 삼십; 9.30 p.m.
Thursday 5th May, **d** 천구백구십구, 삼십; 30th November 1999,
e 화요일, 열, 이십분 전; 20 minutes to 10 in the evening (9.40 p.m.)
Tuesday, **f** 삼, 십구, 두; 2.17 19th March 2008, **g** 일, 일요일, 십일;
1.11 Sunday 1st January, **h** 천구백칠십사, 유, 이십; 20th June 1974
2 a 2, **b** 1, **c** 3

Reading and writing

1 a 20 years old, **b** 17th October, **c** 18 years old, **d** 28th May, **e** 21 years
old, **f** 9th February, **g** 24 years old, **h** 31st November
2 Refer to passage in question 1 for model answer.
3 a The weather in Korea is bad. It is hot and raining. **b** No. it is not
raining in England. **c** It is snowing in America. **d** It is cool and windy in
France.
4 Refer the example given in question for model answer.

Test yourself

1 a … (year) … 년 … (month) … 월 … (day) … 일, **b** … (hour) … 시 …
(minute) … 분, **c** 날씨가 어때요? **d** 69 예순아홉 육십구, 45 마흔다섯
사십오, 24 스물넷 이십사, 81 여든하나 팔십일

2 a Incorrect. 동생 생일이 언제예요? **b** Correct. **c** Correct. **d** Incorrect.
오늘 날짜가 어떻게 돼요?

3 a pure, **b** Sino, **c** Sino, **d** pure, **e** Sino, **f** Sino

UNIT 4

Traditional markets

a

Conversations

1 Yerin is shopping for juice.

2 a Janghun has two types: apple juice and orange juice. The apple juice
is 800 won per bottle; the orange juice is 750 won per bottle. **b** Yerin buys
two items – two bottles of juice. **c** It is 1,550 won in total. **d** Yerin also asks
for a receipt.

3 a 라면 다섯 가지 있어요. **b** 삼다수 물과 볼빅 물 있어요.
c 한 병에 천이백원이에요. **d** 모두 삼천칠백원이에요.

4 Sample answer: 안녕하세요. 어서오세요.; 아니요 주스 없어요.;
네 과자 있어요. 육백원이에요.; 모두 천구백오십원이에요.
네. 여기 있어요. 고맙습니다. 안녕히 가세요.

5 She buys four items: plain milk, apples, biscuits and a book.

6 a 3 kinds of milk, **b** 200 won, **c** No, **d** It is 28,600 won in total.

7 a 우유 있어요? **b** 일반 우유와 초코 우유하고 딸기 우유 있어요.
c 일반 우유는 얼마예요? **d** 딸기 우유는 한 개에 사백원이에요.
e 일반 우유 한 개 주세요. **f** 책도 한 권 주세요. **g** 여기 있어요.
h 고맙습니다. 안녕히 계세요.

Language discovery

a 사과 주스 한 병하고 오렌지 주스 한 병 주세요.
b 일반 우유와 초코 우유하고 딸기 우유 있어요.
c 일반 우유 한 개 주세요. 그리고 사과하고 과자 주세요. 책도 한
권 주세요.

The particles -하고 and -와 are used here to list items. The word그리고 is
also used.

Practice

1 a 과, **b** 와, **c** 과, **d** 하고, **e** 하고, **f** 와/하고 (both are appropriate),
g 하고, **h** 하고, **i** 그리고, **j** 도, **k** 그리고, **l** 도

2 a 물 네 가지 있어요. 그리고 주스 일곱 가지 있어요. **b** 모두 삼만팔천백원이에요.
c 영수증 주세요. 고맙습니다. **d** 책 열 권과 빵, 우유 한 개하고 주스 두 병 주세요. **e** Q: 어서오세요. 뭘 찾으세요? A: 라면 세 개 주세요.
f Q: 사과 있어요? 얼마예요? A: 사과 세 개에 오천원이에요.

Speaking

Have bread: 빵 있어요? **Cream-filled bread:** 크림빵은 얼마예요?
Breads/milk: 크림빵 세 개 주세요. 그리고 우유도 있어요? **Juice:** 사과 주스 한 병하고 오렌지 주스 한 병 주세요. **Total:** 모두 얼마예요? 영수증도 주세요. **Thanks:** 여기 있어요. 고맙습니다. 안녕히 계세요.

Listening

1 a Yerin asks for apples first. She buys five apples. **b** She also asks for ramen and water. No, she doesn't ask for biscuits. **c** The price difference between the two ramen is 70 won. **d** She buys one bottle of water.
e 17,200 won altogether. Yes, she asks for a receipt.
2 a 9, 5, **b** 2, 4, 8, **c** 1, 1, **d** 1, 3, 0, **e** 5, 5, 1, **f** 8, 0, **g** 6, 6, 4, **h** 2, 0, 3, 1

Reading and writing

1 a F, **b** T, **c** Uncertain, **d** T, **e** Uncertain, **f** F, **g** T, **h** T, **i** F
2 1 two bottles of juice, **2** one (unit of) bread, **3** one packet of ramen,
4 five apples, **5** three volumes of book, **6** receipt
3 Sample answer: 안녕하세요! 물 두병과 라면 세 개 주세요. 우유 한 개와 과자 네 개도 주세요. 그리고 사과 여섯 개하고 영수증도 주세요.

Test yourself

1 a 사과는 얼마예요? 사과 세 개는 얼마예요? 모두 얼마예요?
b 과자 세 개와 물 한 병하고 영수증 주세요. **c** 안녕히 계세요.
안녕히 가세요. **d 1** 세, **2** 한, **3** 열, **4** 네, **5** 구천오십, **6** 이만
2 a and; **b** also, too; **c** and; **d** and
3 a 개, **b** 병, **c** 개, **d** 병, **e** 권, **f** 원

UNIT 5

Dining out

If 잘 먹겠습니다, said before the meal, means *I will eat well*, 잘 먹었습니다 used after a meal will mean *I have eaten well*.

Conversations

1 Minjae gets a table for two people.

2 a Taemin orders two cups of green tea. **b** Minjae wants to eat Bibimbap, rice with seasoned vegetables. Taemin chooses to order Twenjang Jjigae, soy bean paste stew. **c** The restaurant doesn't have any Twenjang Jijgae today. Taemin chooses to eat Bibimbap instead. **d** The final food order is two portions of Bibimbap. **e** The counter -잔 uses the pure Korean number system. The counter -인분 uses the Sino-Korean number system.

3 a 네 명이에요. **b** 저는 비빔밥 먹을래요. 저는 비빔밥 먹을게요.
c 죄송합니다. 오늘 맥주가 없어요.

4 Sample answer: 맥주 두 병과 물 한 잔 주세요. 민재씨 뭐 먹을래요?
저는 된장찌개와 갈비 먹을게요.
비빔밥 일 인분과, 갈비 일 인분하고 된장찌개 일 인분 주세요.
그럼 김밥 먹을게요. 비빔밥 일 인분과, 갈비 일 인분하고 김밥 일 인분 주세요.

5 a Two bottles of beer, one bottle of cola, two portions of Samgyopsal (pork belly) and one portion of Kimchi Jjigae (Kimchi stew). **b** The Samgyopsal is too salty and the Kimchi stew is slightly spicy. **c** Suji offers to cook the dishes for them again.

6 a 음식도 지금 주문할게요. **b** 삼겹살 있어요? **c** 여기 있어요. 맛있게 드세요.

7 a Thank you. I will eat well. **b** Over here please! **c** I'm sorry. Shall we cook it again for you?

Language discovery

a What do you want to eat? I want to eat Bibimbap. I will eat Bibimbap.
b Would you like to order? **c** Shall we cook it again for you? Please do it again for me.

Practice

1 a 을, **b** 를, **c** 를, **d** 를, **e** 을, **f** 를 Sentences **e** and **f** should not be using the object particles as the main verb is 있어요/없어요."
2 a 을래요, **b** 을게요, **c** 을래요, **d** 을까요? **e** 겠어요? **f** 어 주세요.
3 a 비빔밥 먹을래요. 비빔밥 일 인분 주세요. **b** 맥주 마실게요. 맥주 한 잔 주세요. **c** 음료수 주문하시겠어요? 음식도 주문하시겠어요? **d** Q: 음식이 어떠세요? A: 정말 맛있어요. **e** A: 김치 찌개가 싱거워요. 그리고 너무 매워요. B: 다시 해드릴까요?

Speaking

Bulgogi: 불고기 있어요? **Ribs/water:** 갈비 이 인분과 물 한 병 주세요. **Ribs salty:** 갈비가 너무 짜요. **Cook again:** 네. 다시 해주세요. **Thanks:** 정말 맛있어요. 고맙습니다. 안녕히 계세요.

Listening

1 a 4 people: Minjae, Taemin, Sara, Jieun, **b** 4 cups of green tea, **c** 2 portions of Bulgogi, 1 portion of Bibimbap and 1 portion of Kimchi stew, **d** They order a bottle of beer in addition with the food.
2 a False, **b** True, **c** Uncertain, **d** True, **e** True

Reading and writing

1 a Twenjang Jjigae, soy bean paste stew, **b** 3 portions, **c** No, **d** 2 soft drinks (green tea), **e** 1 alcoholic drink (beer), **f** 사만팔천원.
2 a False, **b** True, **c** False, **d** True, **e** False, **f** True
3 Sample answer: 네 된장 찌개 있어요. 일 인분에 오천원이에요. 삼겹살도 있어요. 삼겹살은 일 인분에 칠천원이에요. 사라씨 뭐 먹을래요?
4 Sample answer: 사라씨 저는 . . . (food order) . . . 먹을게요. 그리고 . . . (drink order) . . . 마실래요. 모두 얼마예요? 고마워요!

Test yourself

1 a 몇 분이세요? 이쪽으로 앉으세요. 음료수와 음식 주문하시겠어요? **b** 갈비 삼 인분과 김치 찌개 일 인분과 된장 찌개 이 인분 주세요. 그리고 맥주 두 병하고 녹차 한 잔 주세요. **c** 음식이 정말 맛있어요. 고맙습니다. 잘 먹었습니다. **d** 삼겹살이 너무 짜요. 그리고 비빔밥이 조금 매워요. 다시 해주세요.
2 a 5, **b** 3, **c** 4, **d** 1, **e** 2
3 a C, **b** V, **c** V, **d** C, **e** C, **f** C, **g** C, **h** V

UNIT 6

Finding your way

b subway station exit number 1

Conversations

1 Yes
2 a Between the cinema and department store. **b** Roughly 100 metres away. **c** The supermarket is located across from the bank. **d** Hana supermarket

3 a 근처에 병원이 있어요? 어디에 있어요? **b** 서점과 약국 사이에 있어요. **c** 이 쪽으로 이백 미터 쯤 걸어가시면 거기에 수퍼마켓이 있어요. **d** 백화점 옆에 있어요. **e** 학교는 영화관 건너편에 있어요.
4 Answers will vary.
5 Arirang restaurant
6 a The customer is in front of exit number 2 of Kwanghwamun (광화문) subway station. He can see a bookstore and pharmacy. **b** Junki tells the customer to cross the zebra crossing and turn left. He tells the customer that if one walks about 100 metres to the left there is a crossroad. **c** Junki mentions 뽀글뽀글 (**ppogulppogul**) hair salon. **d** You need to walk around 50 metres from the hair salon to the restaurant. **e** The restaurant is next to the cinema.
7 a What can you see right now? **b** I am in front of exit number 2 of Kwanghwamun station. **c** There is also a zebra crossing next to the pharmacy. **d** Turn left. If you walk about 100 metres there is a crossroad. **e** The restaurant is near the hair salon. **f** Our restaurant is next to the cinema. Can you see Arirang?

Language discovery

a 에, **b** 으로, 면, 에, **c** 에서, 으로

Practice

1 a Walk straight ahead in this direction. **b** There is a bank behind the traffic lights over there. There is a hair salon next to the bank. **c** There are traffic lights in front of the subway station exit number 3. Can you see the post office next to the traffic lights? Go to the post office. **d** From here if you cross the zebra crossing there is a pharmacy. From the pharmacy turn left. **e** There isn't a hospital nearby. There is a pharmacy. If you walk about 200 metres in that direction there is a pharmacy across from the subway station. **f** Is there also a hair salon there?
2 a 근처에 백화점이 있어요? 어디에 있어요? **b** 저기 영화관 보이세요? 영화관 옆에 은행 있어요? 서울 은행이에요? **c** 서점이 어디에 있어요? 서점 근처에 슈퍼마켓이 있어요? **d** 왼쪽으로 가세요. 그리고 백 미터 쯤 걸어가시면 우체국이 있어요. **e** 근처에 약국이 없어요. **f** 병원에서 오른쪽으로 가세요. 오십 미터 쯤 걸어가시면 사거리와 신호등이 있어요. **g** 학교 왼쪽에 미용실이 있어요. 그리고 미용실 뒤에 영화관도 있어요. **h** 강남 지하철 역 이 번 출구 옆에 병원이 있어요.
3 a 으로, 면, **b** 에, 에, **c** 으로, 면, 에, 에서, 으로, 면, 에
4 Exit 5: 지하철 역 오 번 출구 앞에 있어요. **Bookstore:** 네. 서점이 어디에 있어요? 미용실 옆에 있어요, **Bank:** 그럼 은행이 어디에

있어요?, **Post office:** 서점 근처에 우체국이 있어요? **Thanks:**
고맙습니다. 안녕히 계세요.
5 Exit 4: 백화점은 지하철 역 사 번 출구와 서점 사이에 있어요.
Bookstore: 저기 횡단보도를 건너가세요. 오른쪽으로 가세요.
그리고 이백 미터 쯤 걸어가시면 거기에 서점이 있어요. **Bank:**
네 백화점 근처에 은행이 있어요. 은행 이름은 서울 은행이에요.
백화점에서 왼쪽으로 가세요. **Pharmacy:** 은행 왼쪽에는 약국과
학교가 있어요. 그리고 은행 건너편에는 신호등이 있어요.

Speaking and listening

1 a F, **b** T, **c** T, **d** F, **e** F, **f** F, **g** T, **h** F, **i** T, **j** F, **k** T
3 a 3, **b** 1, **c** 4, **d** 2

Reading and writing

1 B
2 Sample answer: 지하철 역 일 번 출구 오른쪽에 백화점과 은행이
있어요. 은행 앞에 횡단보도가 있어요. 횡단보도를 건너가시면
영화관이 있어요. 영화관에서 왼쪽으로 가시면 병원과 신호등이
있어요. 신호등에서 오른쪽으로 가세요. 약국 앞에서 횡단보도를
또 건너가시면 거기에 식당이 있어요. 식당 이름은 아리랑
식당이에요. 슈퍼마켓과 은행 사이에 있어요.

Test yourself

1 a 실례합니다. 근처에 영화관이 있어요? 어디에 있어요? **b** 저기
병원이 보이세요? 그리고 옆에 약국도 보이세요? **c** 백화점과 은행
사이에 미용실이 있어요. 그리고 미용실 앞에 횡단보도와 신호등도
있어요. **d** 이 쪽으로 삼백오십 미터 쯤 걸어가시면 학교가 있어요.
2 a 2, **b** 3, **c** 1
3 -(으)면. -으면 is used if the preceding word ends in a consonant, –면 is
used if the preceding word ends in a vowel.
4 a on the right, **b** from the school, **c** to that direction, **d** if you walk, **e** to
the left (direction), **f** from there, **g** if you cross, **h** opposite

UNIT 7

Transport

Four types of transport: subway, bus, train and taxi.

Conversations

1 The subway is the fastest.
2 a line 2, **b** She must get on at Jamsil (잠실) station. Exit number
5 of Jamsil station is located in front of the restaurant over there.

c bus number 360, **d** The passerby thinks it will take roughly 15 minutes to get to Gangnam (강남) station from Jamsil station.

3 a 부산에 가고 싶어요. 어떻게 가요? **b** 그리고 부산 역에서 내리세요. **c** 부산가는 버스 있어요? **d** 하지만 기차가 제일 빨라요. **e** 멀어요? 강남 역에서 부산 역까지 얼마나 걸려요? **f** 네. 멀어요. 삼십분 쯤 걸려요.

4 Answers will vary.

5 Sarah gets directions for three places: Dongdaemun and Namdaemun markets and Busan.

6 a Sarah must take lines 3 and 1 on the subway to get to Dongdaemun market. She must get on line 3 at Gyeongbokkung (경복궁) station, transfer at Jongno 3-ga (종로3가) station onto line 1 and get off at Dongdaemun (동대문) station. **b** To get to Namdaemun market, Sarah can choose between the bus, subway and taxi. The taxi is the fastest. **c** Sarah wants to go to Busan tomorrow. She should take the train. It will take roughly three hours.

7 a Transfer to line 1 at Jongno 3-ga station. And get off at Dongdaemun station. **b** There aren't any buses. There is only the subway. **c** It is slightly far away. The taxi is faster than the bus or subway.

8 a Sino, **b** pure, **c** Sino, **d** Sino

Language discovery

a 강남에 가고 싶어요. **b** 버스나 지하철로 갈 수 있어요. **c** 지하철을 타야 돼요. 갈아타야 돼요.

a 나, 로, 보다 더, **b** 에서, 까지, **c** 밖에

Practice

1 a 가야 돼요, 타고 싶어요, 보다 더. **b** 나, 로, 갈 수 있어요. **c** 갈아탈 수 있어요 에서, 까지. **d** 타야 돼요, 밖에

2 a You can go by motorbike. The motorbike is faster than the car. It is the fastest. **b** There is only the subway. There are no buses that go to Gangnam. It is too far away. **c** I have to go to the department store tomorrow. I want to get the taxi or the car. **d** If you go by train, it takes approximately three hours from Seoul to Busan. **e** You have to transfer to line 3 at Chungmuro (충무로) station. Then you can go to Anguk (안국). **f** I want to get off here. I have to go to the pharmacy over there.

3 a 하나 슈퍼마켓에 가고 싶어요. 어떻게 가요? **b** 부산에 가야 돼요. 서울 역 가는 지하철이 있어요? **c** 지하철이나 버스로 강남에 갈 수 있어요. 하지만 지하철이나 버스보다 택시가 더 빨라요.

d 압구정에 어떻게 가요? 자전거로 갈 수 있어요? **e** 저기 버스 정류장에서 천삼백번 버스를 타세요. 그리고 신촌 역 앞에서 내리세요. **f** 지하철 사 호선을 타세요. 용산에서 갈아탈 수 있어요. 버스는 없어요. 지하철 밖에 없어요. **g** 잠실 역에서 팔 호선으로 갈아타야 돼요. 그리고 천호 역에서 내려야 돼요. 이십 분 쯤 걸려요. **h** 차가 버스보다 더 빨라요. 하지만 차가 기차보다 더 느려요. **i** 버스 정류장에 가야 돼요. 어떻게 가야 돼요?

Speaking

Rodeo Road: 지하철로 가야 돼요. 삼 호선을 타세요. 그리고 압구정 역에서 내리세요. 압구정 역에서 걸어야 돼요. 지하철 역에서 로데오 거리까지 십 분 쯤 걸려요. **Subway faster:** 버스나 지하철을 탈 수 있어요. 하지만 지하철이 버스보다 더 빨라요. 삼 호선을 타세요. 그리고 경복궁 역에서 내리세요. **Transfer:** 삼 호선을 타야 돼요. 그리고 충무로 역에서 사 호선으로 갈아타야 돼요. 명동 역에서 내리세요. 그리고 지하철 역 삼 번 출구 앞에서 택시를 타세요.

Listening

a Buses number 362 and 62 go to the 63 Building. No, the bus isn't the fastest route. **b** Sarah must transfer onto the bus at Daebang (대방) station, by exit number 6. **c** To get to Lotte World, Sarah must take subway lines 3 and 2. She must get on line 3 at Chungmuro (충무로) station, then transfer to line 2 at Seoul University (서울대입구) station and get off at Jamsil (잠실) station. It takes roughly 50 minutes from Chungmuro to Jamsil. **d** No there aren't any buses going to Lotte World, only the subway. **e** Lotte World is further away than the 63 Building. **f** Yes, Sarah can take the bus. No, it is not the recommended route since it is too slow. The subway is faster than the bus. Sarah has to take line 3 and transfer to line 6 at Yaksu (약수) station. **g** The best mode of transportation to get to Deoksugung Palace is the subway. It is the fastest. **h** Lines 1 and 2 take you to the palace. You have to get off at City Hall (시청) station. **i** From the subway station you have to walk to the palace. It takes roughly five minutes.

Reading and writing

1 a It takes Jinu approximately an hour to get from home to work. **b** Jinu takes the bus first. **c** He gets on the subway at Dongdaemun (동대문) station. **d** His final destination is Oksu (옥수) station, which is on line 3. **e** Jinu's office is located behind exit number 2 of Oksu subway station.

f Jinu can alternatively take just the bus but he doesn't as the subway is faster than the bus. The bus is too slow. **g 1** False, **2** False, **3** True, **4** True

2 See the passage given in question 1 for a model answer.

3 Sample answer: 민지: 서울역에서 기차를 타야 돼요. 수원으로 가는 기차를 타세요. 삼십 분 쯤 걸려요. 그리고 수원역에서 버스로 갈아타세요. 수원 지하철 역 사 번 출구 앞에서 삼십칠 번 버스를 타세요. 역에서 한국 민속촌까지 버스로 이십 분 쯤 걸려요. 지훈: 신사역에서 지하철을 타세요. 삼 호선을 타시면 서울대입구역에서 이 호선으로 갈아탈 수 있어요. 강남역에서 내려야 돼요. 그리고 강남 지하철 역 육 번 출구 앞에서 오백육십 번 버스를 타세요. 역에서 한국 민속촌까지 오십 분 쯤 걸려요.

Test yourself

1 a 도곡에 가고 싶어요. 어떻게 가요? 기차로 갈 수 있어요? **b** 이 버스 정류장에서 신촌 가는 버스 있어요? **c** 잠실 역에서 팔 호선을 타야 돼요. 천호 역에서 오 호선으로 갈아탈 수 있어요. 그리고 올림픽 공원 역에서 내려야 돼요. **d** 기차나 지하철로 가야 돼요. 버스도 있어요. 하지만 수원 역이 멀어요. 기차나 지하철이 버스보다 더 빨라요.

2 a I want to ... **b** I can ... **c** I have to ... / I must ...

3 a -(으)로, **b** 밖에, **c** -보다 더, **d** -에서 ... -까지, **e** -(이)나

4 a car or taxi, **b** There are only trains. **c** from Seoul station to Gangnam station, **d** It is faster than the bicycle. **e** You can go by bus. **f** I want to go by car. **g** You have to get off there. **h** You have to transfer at Anguk. **i** You have to transfer to line 1.

UNIT 8

Hobbies and pastimes

Ten different hobbies are listed in the text: sports, taekwondo, ssirum (Korean folk wrestling), football, basketball, baseball, golf, hiking, computer games and Internet games.

Conversations

1 Mikyung likes reading.

2 a Reading and practising the piano. No, Mikyung does not mention travelling in her hobbies. **b** Jongsu likes football and basketball the most. He also enjoys hiking. **c** Yes, Mikyung likes sports. She enjoys hiking too and often plays tennis. **d** Jongsu likes sports because they are fun and relieve stress. Though he sometimes finds sports slightly tiring, he still likes them. Mikyung likes reading because it is fun. She finds reading really fun.

3 a 제 취미는 요리하는 것과 사진 찍는 것이에요. **b** 저는 배드민턴과 테니스를 제일 좋아해요! 낚시하는 것도 즐겨요. **c** 그리고 농구도 자주 해요. **d** 가끔 정말 힘들지만 즐겨요!

4 Answers will vary.

5 Yes, both Jongsu and Minjun like sports.

6 a Minjun likes baseball the most. He plays baseball every week on Thursday and Saturday. He likes baseball so much because it is really good for his health. **b** Minjun often plays table tennis. He also goes hiking once a month. **c** Jongsu's favourite sport is badminton. Lately (these days) he has been playing badminton every day. This is more frequent than usual as he normally plays badminton once every two days. **d** Jongsu also enjoys fishing and golf. **e** Jongsu goes fishing approximately five times a month. He likes it because it is really fun and when he goes fishing it makes him feel better.

7 a I also like sports! What sports do you like Minjun? **b** I often play table tennis too. Also I go hiking once a month. **c** How often do you play badminton? **d** I play approximately five times a month! When I go fishing it makes me feel better. **e** Minjun, do you play baseball often? **f** I play baseball every Thursday and Saturday. It is really good for one's health.

Language discovery

a 재미있고 스트레스가 풀려요! **b** 가끔 조금 힘들지만 좋아해요! –(하)는 것. It effectively means *-ing* in English, changing verbs into nouns.

a 한 달에 한 번 등산을 해요! **b** 하지만 보통 이틀에 한 번 쳐요. **c** 한 달에 다섯 번 쯤 해요! **d** 네 매주 목요일과 토요일에 야구 해요.

Practice

1 a 매주, 힘들지만, **b** 한 달에 다섯 번, 기분이 좋아지고, 낚시하는 것, **c** 매일

2 a What do you do in your free time? Do you like baseball? **b** I take photos every day. Taking photos is really fun. **c** I play computer games once every two days. Though it's fun, it's hard. **d** These days I often go travelling. It is exciting and makes me feel better. **e** I enjoy playing badminton. It makes me fit. It also relieves stress. **f** I enjoy reading books but I like listening to music the most. **g** I dislike table tennis. It is tiring and difficult. It's not for me. **h** I like doing sports. It makes me fit and it is exciting. I do sports every week.

3 a 매주 책을 읽어요. 그리고 매일 피아노 연습을 해요. **b** 골프 치는 것을 좋아해요. 스트레스가 풀려요. **c** 요즘 우표를 모아요.

그리고 가끔 요리를 해요. **d** 농구를 즐겨요. 건강에 좋고
재미있어요. **e** 테니스를 싫어해요. 신나지만 너무 힘들고 어려워요.
f 운동 자주 해요. 이틀에 한 번 축구 해요. 일주일에 두 번 골프
쳐요. **g** 낚시를 싫어해요. 지루하고 재미없어요. **h** 운동 얼마나 자주
해요? 농구와 야구 좋아해요?

Speaking

Like sports: 운동 좋아해요. 탁구와 배드민턴 쳐요. **Exciting/stress:**
신나고 스트레스가 풀려요. 그리고 정말 재미있어요! **Play three
times a week:** 보통 매주 쳐요. 하지만 요즘 일주일에 세 번 쳐요.
Football: 아니요 축구 싫어해요. **Table tennis:** 저랑 안 맞아요.
축구보다 탁구가 더 신나요. 그리고 축구는 너무 힘들어요.

Listening

1 a (like) reading books, listening to music; (dislike) hiking, **b** (like) football,
basketball, tennis; (dislike) fishing, **c** (like) practising the piano; (dislike)
sports, table tennis, baseball, **d** (like) cooking, taking photos; (dislike)
computer games

2 a Suji's hobbies are listening to music, collecting stamps and travelling.
She enjoys travelling the most because it makes her feel better and it
is really exciting. **b** Suji likes hiking but she finds sports tiring in general.
c Jiho likes all sports – baseball, basketball, football, table tennis etc.
He likes tennis too but he finds it a little difficult. **d** Jiho plays football
every day and plays basketball once every two days.

Reading and writing

1 a Minki dislikes sports. He says they are too tiring and not for him.
b Minki likes reading books and travelling because it is fun and exciting.
c Yes he likes watching films too because it makes him feel better. **d** He
normally watches films twice a month. He is watching more films these
days as he is now watching them every week.

2 Sample answer: Hello Martin! What are your hobbies, Martin? What do
you do in your free time? I dislike sports. They are too tiring and not for
me. I like reading books more than sports. Also I enjoy travelling. It is fun
and exciting! I go travelling roughly two times a year. I really like watching
films too. If I watch a film it makes me feel better. I watch films every
week. Normally I watch films roughly twice a month. However these days
I watch them every week! Martin, do you like films too?

3 See the text for question 1 for an example.

Test yourself

1 a 취미가 뭐예요? 우표 모으는 것을 좋아해요? **b** 골프 치는 것과 그림 그리는 것을 즐겨요. 스트레스가 풀려요. **c** 운동을 싫어해요. 건강에 좋지만 너무 힘들고 지루해요.
d 이틀에 한 번 야구를 해요. 기분이 좋아져요. **e** 보통 요리하는 것과 책 읽는 것을 좋아해요. 하지만 요즘 매일 피아노 연습을 해요.

2 a 3, **b** 1, **c** 2

3 a every (week) Sunday, **b** roughly 10 times a year, **c** every (day) morning, **d** once every two days, **e** every year, **f** once every few days, **g** four times a week, **h** roughly seven times a month

UNIT 9

Daily life

Four places of work and study are mentioned: office, school, after-class tutoring academy and university.

Conversations

1 No, neither Minsu nor Cholmin played football yesterday.
2 a Cholmin went hiking yesterday with Jungki. **b** Minsu cleaned and did the laundry in the morning yesterday. He found it really tiring.
c Minsu had lunch with his younger sister Minji. **d** No, Minsu was not busy in the afternoon. He listened to music after lunch.
3 a 그저께 뭐 했어요? **b** 어디서 운동했어요? 언제 운동했어요?
c 저는 오전에 출근했어요. 회사 갔어요. **d** 저녁에는 뭐 했어요? **e** 그 다음에 친구 만났어요. 바빴어요.
4 Answers will vary.
5 Cholmin woke up earlier than Minsu.
6 a Cholmin went to school after he woke up. At school he studied and read books. **b** Minsu woke up at 9 o'clock. Minsu met his friend in the morning. **c** Minsu had lunch with Anna. They met at the department store. **d** No, Minsu was free in the afternoon. He drew pictures at home.
e Cholmin played golf with his older brother.
7 a I woke up at 7 o'clock in the morning. **b** I studied at school. I also read books. **c** I ate lunch with Anna. **d** I was at home. I drew pictures at home. **e** I played golf in the afternoon.
8 Answers will vary.

Language discovery

a 운동했어요. **b** 집에 있었어요. **c** 점심 먹었어요. **d** 음악 들었어요.
a 에, 에서, **b** 에, 에, **c** 에서, 에; -에 is used after a time; -에서 is used after a place.

Practice

1 a 에서, 에, **b** 에, 에서, 에, **c** 에, 에서, 에, **d** 에, 에서
2 a -여요, 공부해요, **b** -아요, 놀아요, **c** -아요, 일어나요, **d** -아요,
만나요, **e** -여요, 등산해요, **f** -어요, 서요, **g** -아요, 봐요, **h** -여요,
요리해요, **i** -였어요, 공부했어요, **j** -았어요, 놀았어요, **k** -았어요,
일어났어요, **l** -았어요, 만났어요, **m** -였어요, 등산했어요, **n** -었어요,
섰어요, **o** -았어요, 봤어요, **p** -였어요, 요리했어요
3 a 오늘 아침 일곱시에 출근했어요. **b** 오후에 식당에서 친구
만났어요. 제인과 함께 저녁 먹었어요. 재미있었어요. **c** 학교에서
음악 들었어요. 그 다음에 책도 읽었어요. **d** 지난주에 벤과 함께
골프 쳤어요. 힘들었어요. **e** 어제 혼자서 집에서 공부했어요.
그 다음에 빨래했어요. 그리고 여섯시에 저녁 먹었어요. 정말
바빴어요. **f** 그저께 저녁 열시에 퇴근했어요.

Speaking

Saturday: 토요일에는 한가했어요. 집에 있었어요. 그리고
청소했어요. **Sunday:** 일요일에는 친구 만났어요. 수잔과 함께
식당에서 점심 먹었어요. **Golf:** 그 다음에 오후 3시에 골프 쳤어요.
정말 재미있었어요. 피터씨는 지난 주말에 뭐 했어요? **Left work:**
토요일에 언제 퇴근했어요?

Listening

1 a F, **b** T, **c** T, **d** F, **e** T, **f** F
2 a Taesu drew pictures and listened to music. He was with his younger
sister. **b** Jongmin went to school with his friend and studied at school. He
said it was not fun. **c** Jongmin played football with his older brother in the
evening yesterday. He said it was really fun.

Reading and writing

1 a Jongmin says he was very busy this past week. **b** Jongmin went to
work on Monday and Tuesday. He went to work at seven in the morning
and left at roughly eight in the evening. He ate his lunch and dinner at
the office during these days. **c** Jongmin played table tennis with his older
sister in the morning on Wednesday. In the afternoon he went hiking on

his own. **d** Yes Jongmin stayed at home on Thursday. He cleaned on his own and also cooked at home. **e** Jongmin met his friend on Friday. They ate lunch together at a restaurant and took pictures at the department store.

2 Hello! What did you do last week, Thomas? Were you busy? I was really busy. On Monday and Tuesday I went to work. I went to work at seven in the morning and left at around eight o'clock in the evening. It was so tiring. I ate lunch and dinner at the office. Did you work too, Thomas? What time did you leave work? On Wednesday I did sports. In the morning I played table tennis with my older sister and in the afternoon I went hiking on my own. Did you do sports too last week, Thomas? On Thursday I stayed at home. I cleaned on my own and I also cooked at home too. It was fun! Also on Friday I met a friend. I ate lunch with my friend in a restaurant and we took pictures at the department store.

3 See the email in question 1 for example.

Test yourself

1 a 그저께 밤에 뭐 했어요? **b** 학교에서 그림 그렸어요. 재미있었어요. **c** 집에 있었어요. 그리고 집에서 혼자서 요리했어요. **d** 어제 저녁에 언제 잤어요? **e** 오전 여덟시에 친구와 함께 출근했어요.

2 a 1, **b** 3, **c** 2

3 a -았어요, 받았어요 **b** -여요, 인사해요 **c** -었어요, 밀었어요 **d** -어요, 읽어요 **e** -여요, 노래해요 **f** -았어요, 앉았어요 **g** -어요, 먹어요 **h** -었어요, 읽었어요

UNIT 10

Weekends, Making appointments to meet

Gangnam, a popular area for Koreans to meet up, is also the setting to Psy's global hit single 'Gangnam Style'.

Conversations

1 No, Yongsu only has plans for Saturday.

2 a Yongsu is meeting his friend in front of exit number 3 at Gangnam station. **b** Yongsu has no appointments on Sunday. He is free. **c** Haeri suggests they meet up on Sunday. **d** Haeri and Yongsu agree to meet at 2 o'clock in front of the department store.

3 a 화요일에 뭐 할 거예요? **b** 토요일에 시간 없어요. **c** 학교 앞에서 만날 거예요. **d** 일요일에 약속 있어요. 바빠요. **e** 저녁 일곱시에 식당 앞에서 만나요!

4 Answers will vary.

5 Jisu and Dana are meeting up on the Wednesday.

6 a Dana has something to do on Thursday. She will be going to school that day. **b** Jisu suggests they meet up at Sinchon station. Dana suggests meeting up at the bus stop. **c** Jisu suggests they go see a football match on Wednesday. Dana says no because she doesn't like football. **d** Jisu and Dana eventually agree to watch a film. **e** Dana suggests they go to a coffee shop in the evening. **f** They will meet at half past four.

7 a When shall we meet next week? **b** Sounds good. I do have time. Let's meet on Wednesday! **c** What shall we do on Wednesday? **d** Let's go watch a football match! How does it sound? **e** Yes I like watching films. Shall we watch a film? **f** See you then! Goodbye!

Language discovery

a 주말에 뭐 할 거예요? **b** 친구 만날 거예요. **c** 그럼 일요일에 만날까요? **d** 영화 볼까요?

a 수요일에 만나요! **b** 축구 경기 보러 가요! **c** 영화 봐요!

Practice

1 a 먹을 거예요. **b** 만날까요? **c** 보러 가요. **d** 있을까요? **e** 먹어요 **f** 갈 거예요

2 a 목욕탕에 갈 거예요; I will go to the public baths. **b** 우표 모을 거예요; I will collect stamps. **c** 그림 그릴 거예요; I will draw pictures. **d** 놀이동산에 놀러 갈 거예요; I will go to a theme park. **e** 배드민턴 칠 거예요; I will play badminton. **f** 여행 할 거예요; I will go travelling. **g** 미술관 갈 거예요; I will go to the gallery. **h** 극장에서 영화 볼 거예요; I will watch a play at the theatre.

3 a 점심 먹을까요? **b** 목욕탕 갈까요? **c** 다나씨랑 놀까요? **d** 여기 앉을까요? **e** 책 읽을까요? **f** 등산하러 갈까요? **g** 음악 들을까요? **h** 기차 탈까요?

4 a 내일 영화 보러 갈 거예요. 친구와 함께 갈 거예요. **b** 지수씨 다음주 주말에 뭐 할 거예요? 토요일에 만날까요? **c** 오늘 저녁 일곱시 반에 아리랑 식당에서 저녁 먹을까요? **d** 월요일에 박물관 가요! 어때요? **e** 금요일에 일 있어요. 학교에서 공부할 거예요.

Speaking

Museum: 네 약속 있어요. 바빠요. 금요일 저녁에는 친구 만날 거예요. 그리고 토요일에는 박물관 갈 거예요. **With mother:** 어머니와 함께 박물관 갈 거예요. **Meet Richard:** 아니요 약속 없어요. 집에 있을 거예요. 리차드씨는 일요일에 뭐 할 거예요?

저녁 먹을까요? **At restaurant:** 좋아요! 일곱시에 식당 앞에서 만나요!

Listening

1 a 2, **b** 3, **c** 4, **d** 1

2 a Minjae and Hojin decide to meet the day after tomorrow. They can't meet tomorrow because Hojin is busy tomorrow – he has something to do. **b** They will meet in the evening as Minjae will go to the office in the morning. **c** They agree to eat dinner at Arirang restaurant and then watch a film in the night. **d** They will meet at half past six in front of the bank situated opposite Seoul station.

Reading and writing

1 a Kanghun suggests they meet on Thursday. **b** Kanghun suggests they eat Bibimbap for dinner near Jamsil. He then proposes going to a coffee shop or the cinema afterwards. **c** Kanghun will be at home on Thursday morning. At night he will go to do sports. **d** Kanghun will go to the office on Wednesday and the public baths on Friday. **e** No, Kanghun has no appointments during the weekend. He will stay at home. He will clean at home and listen to music.

2 Hello Robert! Are you free next Thursday? Are you busy? If you don't have any plans shall we meet? Let's go to eat dinner! Let's eat Bibimbap at a restaurant near Jamsil. And then afterwards let's go to a coffee shop or the cinema! Shall we meet at around seven in the evening? Where shall we meet?

I will be at home in the morning on Thursday. And in the night I will go do sports. So I only have time in the evening. On Wednesday I will go to the office. And on Friday I also have something to do. I will go to the public baths with a friend. However I have no plans at the weekend. I will be at home during the weekend too. I will clean at home. And I will listen to music. So when shall we meet?

3 See the email in question 1 for an example.

Test yourself

1 a 다음주 월요일에 뭐 할 거예요? 약속 있어요? **b** 이미 약속 있어요. 일 있어요. **c** 운동하러 갈 거예요. 그리고 축구 경기 보러 갈 거예요. **d** 내일 오후 세시에 학교 앞에서 만날까요? **e** 마틴과 함께 극장에서 연극 봐요! **f** 쇼핑 할까요? 백화점 뒤에서 봐요!
2 a 1, **b** 3, **c** 7, **d** 4 **e** 6, **f** 2, **g** 5, **h** 8, **i** 9

R1 (UNITS 1–3)

1 a Pakistan, **b** Mexico, **c** New Zealand, **d** Netherlands, **e** Sweden,
f Denmark, **g** Indonesia, **h** Poland, **i** Canada, **j** Singapore
2 a 이에요, **b** 예요, **c** 이세요, **d** 세요, **e** 이에요, **f** 이에요, **g** 이세요,
h 예요
3 a 일곱, **b** 서른여덟, **c** 오십오, **d** 이천십삼, **e** 세, **f** 유, **g** 이십일,
h 천구백구십육
4 a 20 years old. Eden's exact date of birth is 17th December 1994.
b 20 years old. Thomas was born in 1994. **c** 우리 여동생도 생일이
십이월이에요. **d** 5 people: his parents, Thomas, his older sister and his
younger sister. Jenna is his younger sister. **e** 4 people. Eden's sister is
an office worker. She is older than Eden. **f** False, he is called Bill Gerrard.
g American. He is a civil servant. **h** The weather is bad in England. It is
raining. **i** Thomas is in Korea. The weather is warm in Korea.

R2 (UNITS 4–6)

1 a i 하고/와, **ii** 하고/와, **iii** 도, **b i** 하고/과, **ii** 그리고, **c i** 하고/과,
ii 그리고, **d i** 하고/와, **ii** 도, **e i** 하고/와, **ii** 그리고
2 a Turn left. There is a pharmacy next to the school. **b** If you walk
approximately 100 metres in this direction there is a restaurant. **c** Turn
right in front of the school.
d In between the number 2 subway exit and hospital there is a cinema.
e If you cross the zebra crossing there is a department store next to the
restaurant.
3 a iii, **b** i, **c** ii, **d** iv
v: 비빔밥 먹을까요? 저는 비빔밥을 먹을게요.
vi: 저는 갈비를 먹을래요. 그리고 김치찌개도 먹을게요.
4 a 만오천삼십팔 원, **b** 오천사백 원, **c** 이십구만육백 원,
d 사만칠천칠백 원, **e** 육천이백팔십 원, **f** 구만구천구백구십구 원,
g 삼백팔십사만오천이십 원, **h** 칠백사십이만삼백팔십 원
5 a 62, pure, **b** 45, Sino-Korean, **c** 79, Sino-Korean, **d** 45, pure, **e** 17, pure,
f 93, Sino-Korean, **g** 99, pure, **h** 43, Sino-Korean, **i** 88, Sino-Korean
6 a 오십, **b** 스물 여섯, **c** 열아홉, **d** 서른한, **e** 여섯, **f** 팔만오천칠십,
g 일곱
7 a Taksu's restaurant is called Arirang. **b** Somi orders Bulgogi. She
orders two portions. **c** Somi asks for Soy bean paste stew, but Taksu
doesn't sell it. He sells Kimchi stew instead. **d** Somi orders three different
kinds of dishes in total: Bibimbap, Bulgogi and Kimchi stew. **e** The final

bill is 36,000 won. **f** False. The restaurant is located in between Hana supermarket and Do-Re-Mi pharmacy. **g** No, Somi doesn't know where Do-Re-Mi pharmacy is. **h** 압구정 역 삼 번 출구에서 왼쪽으로 가세요. **i** The cinema is located opposite the hospital. (Taksu explains that if you cross the zebra crossing in front of the hospital, there is a cinema) **j** Do-Re-Mi pharmacy is roughly 50 metres away from the cinema.

8 See the reviews in the question to see a model answer.

9 Hyemi buys two bottles of orange juice, one bottle of strawberry milk, one cream bun (크림 빵) and three sweet red bean buns (단팥빵). The total was 5,450 won.

R3 (UNITS 7–10)

1 a Though it's tiring and boring, it is good for your health. **b** I do sports every week. These days I do sports three times a week. **c** Let's meet at 8 o'clock in the evening in front of the restaurant. **d** It takes roughly 15 minutes from Apgujeong to Gangnam. It is closer than Gwanghwamun. **e** You have to take the bus from Seoul Station. There are only buses. There aren't any subways that go there. **f** Going by bus is the fastest. **g** I go hiking five times a month. It is fun and relieves stress.

2 a iii, **b** vii, **c** x, **d** iv, **e** i, **f** ix, **g** vi

ii: 저기서 버스 탈 수 있어요. 지하철도 있어요. **v:** 여기서 갈아탈까요? 옥수에서 갈아타야 돼요? **viii:** 저녁에 만날 수 있어요? 오늘 학교 갈까요? **xi:** 농구 하고 싶어요! 지금 할까요?

3 a 갔어요, **b** 갈 거예요, **c** 먹어요, **d** 먹을 거예요, **e** 그렸어요, **f** 그릴 거예요, **g** 놀아요, **h** 놀았어요, **i** 마셨어요, **j** 마실 거예요, **k** 봐요, **l** 볼 거예요, **m** 좋아해요, **n** 좋아했어요, **o** 앉아요, **p** 앉을 거예요, **q** 입어요, **r** 입을 거예요, **s** 말했어요, **t** 말할 거예요, **u** 줬어요, **v** 줄 거예요, **w** 읽어요, **x** 읽었어요, **y** 섞어요, **z** 섞을 거예요

4 a Yes; he likes baseball and football, as well as badminton. **b** Twice a week these days. He plays football nearly every day. **c** Bongsoon: too tiring and difficult. Wansoo: tiring but fun and good for your health. **d** Because it is exciting and relieves stress. No, she doesn't play baseball; she likes watching it. **e** Nearly every week. Yes, she went last weekend too. **f** Bongsoon went to watch a baseball match on Saturday afternoon. Then she met her friend in the evening. **g** No; she stayed at home and cleaned. Wansoo also stayed at home on Sunday. **h** Wansoo played football with his friends on Saturday morning. In the evening he had dinner with his friends. He was with five friends.

5 a He goes to work Monday–Thursday and has an appointment on Friday. Donju cannot meet up Saturday because he has an appointment. **b** Sunday. **c** Watch a film. The final plan for the entire day is to watch a film and then go to the restaurant nearby to eat dinner. **d** They will meet at 4.00 p.m. in front of the cinema. The cinema is only 5 minutes away from Apgujeong station. **e** Dongju must take line 3 on the subway to get to Apgujeong. **f** Yes, the number 456 or the 420. It takes about 40 minutes to get to Apgujeong by bus. **g** Jimin recommends the subway because the bus is very slow. The subway is the quickest route.

Korean–English glossary

Here is a list of all the Korean vocabulary included in the book. The Korean words have been listed alphabetically. If necessary, look back to the introduction to Hangeul at the front of the book to find the alphabetical order for consonants and vowels.

Here are some simple steps to follow when looking up your Korean word:

▶ Take the first syllable block of the word. Observe its letters.
▶ Look up the letters in chronological order. The first letter will always be a consonant, the second will always be a vowel, and if there is a third letter this will be another consonant.

가격	*price*
가까워요	*is close*
가끔	*sometimes*
가을	*autumn*
가족	*family*
갈비	*beef/pork ribs*
갈아타요	*transfer*
강남	*Gangnam (place name)*
강남역	*Gangnam station*
-개	*- items (basic counting unit)*
거기	*there*
건강에 좋아요	*is good for one's health*
건강해져요	*become fit*
건너가요	*cross*
건너편	*opposite*
걸려요	*take (period of time)*
걸어가요	*walk*
게임방	*gaming arcade, gaming rooms*
겨울	*winter*
결혼	*marriage*
결혼했어요	*is married*
계란	*egg*
계산서	*bill*
계절	*season*
고려대학교	*Korea University*
고맙습니다	*thank you*

골프	golf
골프쳐요	play golf
공공 건물	public buildings
공무원	civil servant
공부해요	study
-과	and
과자	biscuits
관광객	tourist
관광지	tourist attraction
교수	professor
교육	education
교통	transport
교통 카드	transportation card
구	nine (Sino-Korean)
구백	nine hundred (Sino-Korean)
구십	ninety (Sino-Korean)
구월	September
국	soup
-권	books (counter)
그 다음	afterwards
그 전	before that
그래서	and so
그려요	draw (pictures)
그리고	and, also
그림	picture
그저께	day before yesterday
극장	theatre
근처	near
금요일	Friday
기분이 좋아져요	get (to) feel better
기차	train
김치	kimchi
김치찌개	kimchi stew
나빠요	is bad
나이	age
낚시	fishing
날짜	date
남동생	younger brother
남산 타워	Namsan Tower
남편	husband
낮	daytime
내리다	get off

내일	*tomorrow*
너무	*too, exceedingly*
넷	*four (pure Korean)*
녹차	*green tea*
놀이공원	*theme park*
농구	*basketball*
누구	*who*
누나	*boy's older sister*
눈이 와요	*is snowing*
느려요	*is slow*
다섯	*five (pure Korean)*
다시	*again*
다음주 (주말)	*next week (weekend)*
달력	*calendar*
당일치기 여행	*day trip*
대가족	*extended family*
대중 교통	*public transport*
대학생	*university student*
대한민국	*South Korea*
더워요	*is hot*
도로	*road*
도시	*city*
독일 사람	*German (person)*
동대문 시장	*Dongdaemun Market*
동대문 역	*Dongdaemun station*
동시통역	*simultaneous interpretation*
된장찌개	*soy bean paste stew*
둘	*two (pure Korean)*
뒤	*behind*
들어요	*listen*
등산	*hiking*
등산해요	*go hiking*
따뜻해요	*is warm*
딸	*daughter*
딸기 우유	*strawberry-flavoured milk*
또	*again*
똑바로	*straight ahead*
라면	*ramen*
러시아 사람	*Russian (person)*
로데오 거리	*Rodeo Road*
마흔	*forty (pure Korean)*
만	*ten thousand (Sino-Korean)*

만나요	*meet*
많이	*many, a lot*
많이 파세요!	*Sell lots!*
맑아요	*is clear*
맛있어요	*is tasty*
매달	*every month*
매워요	*is spicy*
매일	*every day*
매주	*every week*
맥주	*beer*
먹어요	*eat*
멀어요	*is far away*
명함	*namecard, business card*
몇 시예요?	*What time is it?*
모레	*day after tomorrow*
모아요	*collect*
목요일	*Thursday*
목욕탕	*public baths*
목적지	*destination*
물	*water*
물건 사기	*shopping*
미국 사람	*American (person)*
미술관	*gallery*
미용실	*hair salon*
바람이 불어요	*is windy*
바빠요	*busy*
박물관	*museum*
박세리	*Se-Ri Park (golfer)*
박지성	*Ji-Sung Park (footballer)*
박찬호	*Chan-Ho Park (baseballer)*
반가워요.	*Nice to meet you.*
반찬	*side dish*
밤	*night*
밥	*rice*
배	*pear*
배드민턴	*badminton*
백	*one hundred (Sino-Korean)*
백화점	*department store*
버스	*bus*
버스 정류장	*bus stop*
-번 출구	*exit number ...*
변호사	*lawyer*

-병	bottles (counter)
병원	hospital
보통	normally
봄	spring
봐요	see, watch
부모님	parents
부부	husband and wife
부산	Busan (place name)
분	people (honorific counter)
불고기	marinated beef BBQ
비가 와요	is raining
비누	soap
비빔밥	rice with seasoned vegetables
비싸요	expensive
빨라요	is fast
빨래	laundry
빨래해요	do laundry
빵	bread
사	four (Sino-Korean)
사거리	crossroad
사과	apple
사과 주스	apple juice
사람	person
사백	four hundred (Sino-Korean)
사십	forty (Sino-Korean)
사월	April
사이	in between
사진	photo
사진 찍어요	take photos
삼	three (Sino-Korean)
삼겹살	pork belly
삼백	three hundred (Sino-Korean)
삼십	thirty (Sino-Korean)
삼월	March
상사	superior (in the office)
생일	birthday
서른	thirty (pure Korean)
서울	Seoul
서울대학교	Seoul National University
서울역	Seoul station
서점	book store
선배	senior

선생님	teacher
설날	Chinese new year
성	surname
성함	name (honorific word)
셋	three (pure Korean)
손님	customer
쇼핑	shopping
쇼핑몰	shopping mall
쇼핑해요	go shopping
수도	capital
수요일	Wednesday
수원역	Suwon station
숟가락	spoon
쉰	fifty (pure Korean)
슈퍼마켓	supermarket
스물	twenty (pure Korean)
스위스 사람	Swiss (person)
스트레스가 풀려요	relieves stress
시간	time
시원해요	is cold
시월	October
식당	restaurant
식사	meal
신나요	is exciting
신사역	Sinsa station
신호등	traffic lights
실례합니다	excuse me
싫어해요	dislike
십	ten (Sino-Korean)
십만	hundred thousand (Sino-Korean)
십이월	December
십일월	November
싱거워요	is bland
싸요	is cheap
-씨	(title) Mr/Mrs
씨름	ssirum (Korean folk wrestling)
아내	wife
아니요	no
아들	son
아버지	father
아이	child
아침	breakfast, morning

아홉	*nine (pure Korean)*
아흔	*ninety (pure Korean)*
악수	*handshake*
안녕하세요	*hello*
안녕히 가세요	*goodbye*
앉으세요.	*Please sit.*
압구정	*Apgujeong (place name)*
앞	*(in) front*
야구	*baseball*
약국	*pharmacy*
약속	*appointment*
약수터	*mineral spring*
양력	*solar (calendar)*
어디서	*where*
어때요?	*How is it?*
어려워요	*is difficult*
어머니	*mother*
어서오세요!	*Welcome!*
어제	*yesterday*
언니	*girl's older sister*
언제	*when*
얼마예요?	*How much is it?*
업무	*task*
없어요	*don't have*
여기	*here*
여기요!	*Over here, please!*
여덟	*eight (pure Korean)*
여동생	*younger sister*
여든	*eighty (pure Korean)*
여름	*summer*
여섯	*six (pure Korean)*
여행	*travelling*
역	*station*
연극	*play*
연세	*age (honorific word)*
연세대학교	*Yonsei Univeristy*
열	*ten (pure Korean)*
영국 사람	*British (person)*
영수증	*receipt*
영화	*film*
영화관	*cinema*
옆	*next to*

예	*yes*
예순	*sixty (pure Korean)*
예의	*respect*
오	*five (Sino-Korean)*
오늘	*today*
오랜만이에요!	*Long time no see!*
오렌지 주스	*orange juice*
오른쪽	*right*
오백	*five hundred (Sino-Korean)*
오빠	*girl's older brother*
오십	*fifty (Sino-Korean)*
오월	*May*
오전	*a.m.*
오토바이	*motorbike*
오후	*p.m.*
옥수	*Oksu (place name)*
-와	*and*
왼쪽	*left*
요리	*cooking*
요리사	*chef*
요리해요	*do cooking*
요즘	*these days*
우유	*milk*
우체국	*post office*
우표	*stamp*
운동	*sports*
운동해요	*do sports*
운전기사	*driver*
월요일	*Monday*
위치	*location*
유월	*June*
유적지	*place of historic interest*
육	*six (Sino-Korean)*
육백	*six hundred (Sino-Korean)*
육십	*sixty (Sino-Korean)*
은행	*bank*
음력	*lunar (calendar)*
음료수	*drink*
음식	*food*
음악	*music*
의사	*doctor*
이	*two (Sino-Korean)*

이 쪽으로	in this direction
이름	first name
이백	two hundred (Sino-Korean)
이십	twenty (Sino-Korean)
-이에요/예요	is
이월	February
이태원	Itaewon
-인분	-portions (counter)
인사해요	say hello
인터넷 게임	Internet game
일	work
일	one (Sino-Korean)
일곱	seven (pure Korean)
일반 우유	plain milk
일본 사람	Japanese (person)
일어나요	wake up, get up
일요일	Sunday
일월	January
일해요	do work
일흔	seventy (pure Korean)
읽어요	read
있어요	have
자동차	car
자요	sleep
자전거	bicycle
자주	often
-잔	-glasses (counter)
장남	eldest son
장마	monsoon
장소	location/place
재미없어요	is not fun
재미있어요	is fun
저 쪽으로	in that direction
저기	over there
저녁	dinner, evening
저랑 안 맞아요	is not for me
전단지	leaflet
전통시장	traditional market
전화	phone
절	temple
점심	lunch, lunchtime
젓가락	chopsticks

정말	*very, really*
조금	*slightly*
종로 삼가	*Jongro 3-ga (place name)*
좋아요	*is good*
좋아해요	*like*
죄송합니다.	*I'm sorry.*
주말	*weekend*
주문해요	*order*
주부	*housewife*
주세요	*please give (me)*
주소	*address*
주스	*juice*
중국 사람	*Chinese (person)*
중독	*addiction*
즐겨요	*enjoy*
지금	*now*
지난 주말	*last weekend*
지난주	*last week*
지도	*map*
지루해요	*is boring*
지하철	*subway*
지하철 역	*subway stations*
직업	*occupation*
집	*home*
짜요	*is salty*
쯤	*approximately*
찌개	*stew*
찍어요	*take (photos)*
책	*book*
천	*thousand (Sino-Korean)*
청소	*cleaning*
청소해요	*clean up*
초코 우유	*chocolate-flavoured milk*
추석	*Harvest festival*
추워요	*is cold*
축구	*football*
축구 경기	*football match*
출구 번호	*exit number*
출근해요	*go to work*
취미	*hobby*
치과 의사	*dentist*
친구	*friend*

칠	seven (Sino-Korean)
칠백	seven hundred (Sino-Korean)
칠십	seventy (Sino-Korean)
칠월	July
커피	coffee
커피숍	coffe shop
컴퓨터 게임	computer game
크림빵	cream-filled bread
타요	get on, ride
탁구	table tennis
탁구쳐요	play table tennis
태국 사람	Thai (person)
태권도	taekwondo
택시	taxi
테니스	tennis
토요일	Saturday
퇴근해요	leave work
팔	eight (Sino-Korean)
팔백	eight hundred (Sino-Korean)
팔십	eighty (Sino-Korean)
팔월	August
팥빵	sweet red bean paste bun
프랑스 사람	French (person)
피씨방	Internet café
피아노	piano
하고	and
하나	one (pure Korean)
학교	school
학생	student
학원	after-class tutoring academy
한가해요	be free
한국 민속촌	Korean folk village
한국 사람	Korean (person)
한국 선수	Korean athlete
할머니	grandmother
할아버지	grandfather
해요	do
핵가족	nuclear family
행인	passerby
형	boy's older brother
호주 사람	Australian (person)
혼자서	alone

화요일	Tuesday
환승 할인	transfer discount
회사	office
회사원	office worker
회식	after-work drinks
횡단보도	zebra crossing
휴지	tissue
흐려요	is cloudy
힘들어요	is tiring

Transliteration appendix

Following are the transliterations of the conversations in Units 1–10.

UNIT 1

01.02 Conversation 1

학생1	안녕하세요. 저는 이철수예요.
Haksaeng 1	Annyonghaseyo. Jonun Yi cholsu yeyo.
학생2	안녕하세요. 저는 김상민이에요.
Haksaeng 2	Annyonghaseyo. Jonun Kim sangmin ieyo.
학생1	상민씨, 만나서 반가워요.
Hansaeng 1	Sangmin ssi, Mannaso Pangawoyo.
학생2	철수씨, 만나서 반가워요.
Haksaeng 2	Cholsu ssi Mannaso Pangawoyo.
학생1	다음에 또 봐요. 안녕히 가세요.
Haksaeng 1	Taume tto pwayo. Annyonghi kaseyo.
학생2	안녕히 가세요.
Haksaeng 2	Annyonghi kaseyo.

01.03 Conversation 2

여자	안녕하세요. 저는 최한별이에요.
Yoja	Annyonghaseyo. Jonun Choi hanbyol ieyo.
모두	한별씨, 안녕하세요.
Modu	Hanbyol ssi annyonghaseyo.
여자	저는 한국 사람이에요. 저는 의사예요. 만나서 반가워요.
Yoja	Jonun hanguk saram ieyo. Jonun uisa yeyo. Mannaso pangawoyo.
모두	만나서 반가워요.
Modu	Mannaso pangawoyo.

01.04 Conversation 3

여자	안녕하세요. 만나서 반가워요. 저는 최한별이에요.
Yoja	Annyonghaseyo. Mannaso pangawoyo. Jonun Choe hanbyol ieyo.
지미 스미스	안녕하세요. 저는 지미 스미스예요. 만나서 반가워요.

Jimi sumisu	Annyonghaseyo. Jonun Jimi sumisu yeyo. Mannaso pangawoyo.
여자	지미씨, 어느 나라 사람이에요?
Yoja	Jimi ssi, onu nara saram ieyo?
지미 스미스	저는 미국 사람이에요.
Jimi sumisu	Jonun miguk saram ieyo.
여자	직업은 뭐예요?
Yoja	Jigobun mwo yeyo?
지미 스미스	저는 선생이에요.
Jimi sumisu	Jonun sonsaeng ieyo.

UNIT 2

02.02 Conversation 1

준수	용호씨, 가족이 몇 명이에요?
Junsu	Yonghossi, kajogi myonmyong ieyo?
용호	우리 가족은 네명이에요.
Yongho	Uri kajogun ne myong ieyo.
준수	누구누구예요?
Junsu	Nugu nugu yeyo?
용호	우리 아버지, 어머니, 여동생하고 저예요.
Yongho	Uri aboji, omoni, yodongsaeng hago jo yeyo.
준수	아버지는 성함이 어떻게 되세요?
Junsu	Abojinun songhami ottok^he tweseyo?
용호	최민관이세요. 우리 아버지는 교수세요.
Yongho	Choe minkwan iseyo. Uri abojinun kyosu seyo.
준수	연세가 어떻게 되세요?
Junsu	Yonsega ottok^he tweseyo?
용호	마흔두살이세요.
Yongho	Mahun tusal iseyo.
준수	여동생은 이름이 뭐예요? 그리고 나이가 몇 살이에요?
Junsu	Yodongsaengun irumi mwo yeyo? Kurigo naiga myossal ieyo?
용호	우리 여동생은 최용미예요. 그리고 용미는 열세살이에요.
Yongho	Uri yodongsaengun Choe Yongmi yeyo. Kurigo Yongminun yolsesal ieyo.

02.04 Conversation 2

| 장호 | 민준씨! 오랜만이에요! 인사해요. 우리 아내예요. |
| Jangho | Minjun ssi! Oraenman ieyo! Insahaeyo. Uri anae yeyo. |

수빈	안녕하세요. 저는 최수빈이에요. 만나서 반가워요.
Subin	Annyonghaseyo. Jonun choe subin ieyo. Mannaso pangawoyo.
민준	안녕하세요! 저는 박민준이에요.
Minjun	Annyonghaseyo! Jonun pak minjun ieyo.
장호	*(to his wife)* 민준씨는 교수예요. 그리고 서른다섯살이에요.
Jangho	Minjunssi nun kyosu yeyo. Kurigo sorundasossal ieyo. *(to Minjun)* 민준씨, 결혼 했어요?
	Minjun ssi, kyolhon [kyoron] haessoyo?
민준	예. 결혼 했어요. 아이 두명 있어요. 딸하고 아들 있어요.
Minjun	Ye. Kyolhon haessoyo. Ai tumyong issoyo. Ttal hago adul issoyo.

UNIT 3

03.02 Conversation 1

상수	오늘 몇월 며칠이에요?
Sangsu	Onul myodwol myochil ieyo?
주리	팔월 이십이일이에요.
Juri	Pʰalwol ishibiil ieyo.
상수	무슨 요일이에요?
Sangsu	Musun yoil ieyo?
주리	화요일이에요.
Juri	Hwayoil ieyo.
상수	지금 몇 시예요?
Sangsu	Jigum myossi yeyo?
주리	오후 두시 삼십분이에요.
Jurin	Ohu tushi samship sabun ieyo.
상수	오늘 날씨가 어때요?
Sangsu	Onul nalssiga ottaeyo?
주리	날씨가 좋아요! 따뜻해요. 그리고 맑아요.
Juri	Nalssiga joayo. Ttattutʰaeyo. Kurigo malgayo.

03.04 Conversation 2

상수	주리씨는 생일이 언제예요?
Sangsu	Juri ssi nun saengiri onje yeyo?
주리	제 생일은 사월 오일이에요.
Juri	Je saengirun sawol oil ieyo.

상수	몇년생이에요?
Sangsu	Myonnyon saeng ieyo?
주리	천구백구십일년생이에요. 상수씨는 생일이 언제예요?
Juri	Chongubaek kuship ilnyon saeng ieyo. Sangsu ssi nun saengiri onje yeyo?
상수	제 생일은 이월 이십일일이에요. 그리고 저는 천구백팔십칠년생 이에요.
Sangsu	Je saengirun iwol iship ilil ieyo. Kurigo jo nun chongubaek p^halship chilnyon saeng ieyo.
주리	그럼 상수씨는 몇살이에요?
Juri	Kurom sangsu ssi nun myossal ieyo?
상수	저는 스물여섯살이에요. 주리씨는 몇 살이에요?
Sangsu	Jonun sumul yosossal ieyo. Juri ssi nun myossal ieyo?
주리	저는 스물두살이에요.
Juri	Jonun sumul tusal ieyo.

UNIT 4

04.02 Conversation 1

장훈	안녕하세요. 어서오세요.
Janghun	Annyonghaseyo. Oso oseyo.
예린	안녕하세요. 주스 있어요?
Yerin	Annyonghaseyo. Jusu issoyo?
장훈	네. 주스 두 가지 있어요. 사과 주스와 오렌지 주스 있어요.
Janghun	Ne. jusu tu kaji issoyo. Sagwa jusu wa orenji jusu issoyo.
예린	사과 주스는 얼마예요?
Yerin	Sagwa jusunun olma yeyo?
장훈	한 병에 팔백원이에요.
Janghun	Han byong e p^halbaek won ieyo.
예린	그럼 오렌지 주스는 얼마예요?
Yerin	Kurom orenji jusunun olma yeyo?
장훈	한 병에 칠백오십원이에요.
Janghun	Han byong e chilbaek oship won ieyo.
예린	사과 주스 한 병하고 오렌지 주스 한 병 주세요. 모두 얼마예요?
Yerin	Sagwa jusu han byong hago orenji jusu han byong juseyo. Modu olma yeyo?
장훈	모두 천오백오십원이에요.

Janghun	Modu chon obaek ship won ieyo.
예린	영수증도 주세요.
Yerin	Yongsujungdo juseyo.
장훈	여기 있어요. 고맙습니다. 안녕히 가세요.
Janghun	Yogi issoyo. komapsumnida. Annyonghi kaseyo.
예린	고맙습니다. 안녕히 계세요.
Yerin	Komapsumnida. Annyonghi kyeseyo.

04.04 Conversation 2

두호	어서오세요. 뭘 찾으세요?
Duho	Oso oseyo. Mwol chajuseyo?
예린	안녕하세요. 우유 있어요?
Yerin	Annyonghaseyo. Uyu issoyo?
두호	네. 우유 있어요. 세 가지 있어요. 일반 우유와 초코 우유하고 딸기 우유 있어요.
Duho	Ne. Uyu issoyo. Se kaji issoyo. Ilban uyuwa chok^{h}o uyu hago ttalgi uyu issoyo.
예린	일반 우유는 얼마예요? 그리고 초코 우유하고 딸기 우유는 얼마예요?
Yerin	Ilban uyunun olma yeyo? Kurigo chok^{h}o uyu hago ttalgi uyunun olma yeyo?
두호	일반 우유는 한개에 삼백원, 초코 우유는 오백원, 그리고 딸기 우유는 한 개에 사백원이에요.
Duho	Ilban uyunun han gae e sambaek won, chok^{h}o uyunun obaek won, kurigo ttalgi uyunun han gae e sabaek won ieyo.
예린	일반 우유 한 개 주세요. 그리고 사과하고 과자 주세요. 책도 한 권 주세요. 그럼 모두 얼마예요?
Yerin	Ilban uyu han gae juseyo. Kurigo sagwa hago kwaja juseyo. Chaekto han kwon juseyo. Kurom modu olma yeyo?
두호	모두 이만팔천육백원이에요.
Duho	Modu iman p^{h}alchon yukbaek won ieyo.
예린	여기 있어요. 고맙습니다. 안녕히 계세요.
Yerin	Yogi issoyo. Komapsumnida. Annyonghi kyeseyo.
두호	고맙습니다. 안녕히 가세요.
Duho	Komapsumnida. Annyonghi kaseyo.

UNIT 5

Conversation 1

수지	어서오세요. 몇 분이세요?
Suji	Oso oseyo. Myo ppun iseyo?
민재	두 명이에요.
Minjae	Tu myong ieyo.
수지	이 쪽으로 앉으세요.
Suji	I jjoguro anjuseyo.
민재	고맙습니다.
Minjae	Komapsumnida.
수지	음료수 주문하시겠어요?
Suji	Umnyosu jumun hasigessoyo?
태민	녹차 두 잔 주세요. 민재씨, 뭐 먹을래요?
Taemin	Nokcha tu jan juseyo. Minjae ssi, mwo mogullaeyo?
민재	저는 비빔밥을 먹을래요.
Minjae	Jonun bibimbabul mogullaeyo.
태민	그럼 저는 된장찌개를 먹을게요.
Taemin	Kurom jonun twenjang jjigaerul mogulkkeyo.
수지	음식 주문하시겠어요?
Suji	Umsik jumun hasigessoyo?
태민	비빔밥 일 인분하고 된장찌개 일 인분 주세요.
Taemin	Bibimbap il inbun hago twenjang jjigae il inbun juseyo.
수지	죄송합니다. 오늘 된장찌개가 없어요.
Suji	Joesonghamnida. Onul twenjang jjigaega opssoyo.
태민	그럼 비빔밥 이 인분 주세요.
Taemin	Kurom bibimbap i inbun juseyo.

Conversation 2

수지	음료수 주문하시겠어요?
Suji	Umnyosu jumunhashigessoyo?
민재	네. 맥주 두 병하고 콜라 한 병 주세요.
Minjae	Ne. maekju tu byong hago kʰolla han byong juseyo.
태민	음식도 지금 주문할게요. 삼겹살 있어요?
Taemin	Umshikto jigum jumunhalkkeyo. Samgyopsal issoyo?
수지	네. 삼겹살 있어요.
Suji	Ne. Samgyopsal issoyo.
태민	그럼 삼겹살 이 인분 주세요. 그리고 김치 찌개 일 인분 주세요.

| Taemin | Kurom samgyopsal i inbun juseyo. Kurigo kimchi jjigae il inbun juseyo. |

A while later, Suji brings the order . . .

수지	여기 있어요. 맛있게 드세요.
Suji	Yogi issoyo. Mashikke tuseyo.
민재	고맙습니다. 잘 먹겠습니다.
Minjae	Komapsumnida. Jal mokkessumnida.

After trying the food Taemin calls Suji . . .

태민	여기요!
Taemin	Yogiyo!
수지	네. 음식은 어떠세요?
Suji	Ne. Umsigun ottoseyo?
태민	삼겹살이 너무 짜요. 그리고 김치 찌개가 조금 매워요.
Taemin	Samgyopsari nomu jjayo. Kurigo kimchi jjigaega jogum maewoyo.
수지	죄송합니다. 다시 해드릴까요?
Suji	Joesonghamnida. Tashi haedurilkkayo?
태민	네. 다시 해주세요.
Taemin	Ne. Tashi haejuseyo.

UNIT 6

<u>06.02</u> Conversation 1

태희	실례합니다. 근처에 은행이 있어요?
Taehee	Sillehamnida. Kuncho e unhaengi issoyo?
행인	네, 있어요.
Haengin	Ne, issoyo.
태희	어디에 있어요?
Taehee	Odie issoyo?
행인	저기 영화관 보이세요? 그 뒤에 백화점도 보이세요? 영화관과 백화점 사이에 있어요. 여기서 횡단보도를 건너가세요. 그리고 저 쪽으로 백 미터 쯤 걸어가시면 거기에 은행이 있어요.
Haengin	Jogi yonghwagwan poiseyo? Ku twie paekʰwajomdo poiseyo? Yonghwagwan kwa paekʰwajom saie issoyo. Yogiso hoengdanbodo rul konno kaseyo. Kurigo jo jjoguro paek mitʰo jjum korogasimyon kogie unhaengi issoyo.
태희	고맙습니다. 그리고 슈퍼마켓은 어디에 있어요?
Taehee	Komapsumnida. Kurigo shupʰomakʰesun odie issoyo?

행인	슈퍼마켓은 은행 건너편에 있어요. 하나 슈퍼마켓이에요. 약국 옆에 있어요.
Haengin	Shup^homak^hesun unhaeng konnop^hyone issoyo. Hana shup^homak^het ieyo. Yakkuk yop^he issoyo.
태희	고맙습니다! 안녕히 가세요!
Taehee	Komapsumnida! Annonghi kaseyo!

손님	아리랑 식당이 어디에 있어요?
Sonnim	Arirang sikttangi odie issoyo?
준기	지금 뭐가 보이세요?
Junki	Jigum mwoga poiseyo?
손님	지금 광화문역 이 번 출구 앞에 있어요. 여기에 서점과 약국이 있어요. 약국 앞에 횡단보도도 있어요.
Sonnim	Jigum kwanghwamun yok ibon chulgu ap^he issoyo. Yogie sojom kwa yakkugi issoyo. Yakkuk ap^he hoengdanbododo issoyo.
준기	일단 횡단보도를 건너가세요. 그리고 왼쪽으로 가세요. 백 미터 쯤 걸어가시면 사거리가 있어요.
Junki	Ilttan hoengdanbodorul konno kaseyo. Kurigo oenjjokuro kaseyo. paek mit^ho jjum korogasimyon sagoriga issoyo.
손님	네! 사거리가 있어요.
Sonnim	Ne! sagoriga issoyo.
준기	사거리 건너편에 미용실이 보이세요? 미용실 이름은 뽀글뽀글이에요.
Junki	Sagori konnop^hyone miyongsiri poiseyo? Miyongsil irumun ppogulppogul ieyo.
손님	네! 뽀글뽀글 미용실 앞에 있어요.
Sonnim	Ne! ppogulppogul miyongsil ap^he issoyo.
준기	식당은 미용실 근처에 있어요. 미용실 앞에서 오른쪽으로 가세요. 오십 미터 쯤 가시면 영화관이 있어요. 그리고 영화관 옆에 우리 식당이 있어요. 아리랑 식당이 보이세요?
Junki	Sikttangun miyongsil kunchoe issoyo. Miyongsil ap^heso orunjjoguro kaseyo. Oship mit^ho jjum kasimyon yonghwagwani issoyo. Kurigo yonghwagwan yop^he uri sikttangı ıssoyo. Arirang sikttangi poiseyo?
손님	아 네! 아리랑 식당! 고맙습니다. [enters shop] 안녕하세요.

Sonnim	A ne! arirang sikttang! Komapsumnida. [enters shop] Annonghaseyo.
준기	어서오세요! 몇 분이세요?
Junki	Oso oseyo! Myot pun iseyo?

UNIT 7

07.02 Conversation 1

태희	실례합니다. 강남에 가고 싶어요. 어떻게 가요?
Taehee	Sillehamnida. Gangname kago shipʰoyo. Ottokʰe kayo?
행인	잠실 지하철 역에서 이(2) 호선을 타세요. 그리고 강남 역에서 내리세요.
Haengin	Jamsil jihachol yogeso i hosonul tʰaseyo. Kurigo gangnam yogeso naeriseyo.
태희	잠실 역이 어디에 있어요?
Taehee	Jamsil yogi odie issoyo?
행인	저기 식당 보이세요? 식당 앞에 오(5) 번 출구가 있어요.
Haengin	Jogi sikttang poiseyo? Sikttang apʰe opon chulguga issoyo.
태희	강남 역 가는 버스 있어요?
Taehee	Gangnam yok kanun posuga issoyo?
행인	오 번 출구 옆에 버스 정류장이 있어요. 거기에서 삼백육십번 버스가 강남으로 가요. 하지만 지하철이 제일 빨라요.
Haengin	Obon chulgu yopʰe posu jongnyujangi issoyo. Kogieso sambaek yukship pon bosuga gangnamuro kayo. Hajiman jihachori jeil ppallayo.
태희	멀어요? 잠실 역에서 강남 역까지 얼마나 걸려요?
Taehee	Moroyo? Jamsil yogeso gangnam yok kkaji olmana kollyoyo?
행인	아니요. 가까워요. 십오분 쯤 걸려요.
Haengin	Aniyo. Kakkawoyo. Ship obun jjum kollyoyo.

07.04 Conversation 2

사라	오늘 동대문 시장에 가야 돼요. 어떻게 가요?
Sarah	Onul tongdaemun sijange kaya tweyo. Ottokʰe kayo?
진우	지하철을 타야 돼요. 저기 경복궁 역에서 삼 호선을 타세요.
Jinu	Jihacholul tʰaya tweyo. Jogi kyeongbokkung yogeso sam hosonul tʰaseyo.

사라	갈아타야 돼요?
Sarah	Karatʰaya tweyo?
진우	네 갈아타야 돼요! 종로삼가 역에서 일 호선으로 갈아타세요. 그리고 동대문 역에서 내리세요.
Jinu	Ne karatʰaya tweyo! Jongnosamga yogeso il hosonuro karatʰaseyo. Kurigo tongdaemun yogeso naeriseyo.
사라	동대문 시장 가는 버스도 있어요?
Sarah	Tongdaemun sijang kanun posudo issoyo?
진우	아니요. 버스 없어요. 지하철 밖에 없어요.
Jinu	Aniyo. Posu opssoyo. Jihachol pakke opssoyo.
사라	그럼 남대문 시장에 어떻게 가요?
Sarah	Kurom namdaemun sijange ottokʰe kayo?
진우	버스나 지하철로 갈 수 있어요. 택시도 있어요. 남대문 시장은 조금 멀어요. 버스나 지하철보다 택시가 더 빨라요.
Jinu	Posuna jihachollo kal su issoyo. Tʰaeksido issoyo. Namdaemun sijangun jogum moroyo. Posuna jihacholboda tʰaeksiga to ppallayo.
사라	그리고 내일 부산 가고 싶어요. 부산에 어떻게 가요?
Sarah	Kurigo naeil pusan kago shipʰoyo. Pusane ottokʰe kayo?
진우	기차로 가세요. 세 시간 쯤 걸려요.
Jinu	Kicharo kaseyo. Se sigan jjum kollyoyo.

UNIT 8

08.02 Conversation 1

종수	미경씨, 취미가 뭐예요?
Jongsu	Mikyung ssi, chwimiga mwo yeyo?
미경	제 취미는 책 읽는 것과 피아노 연습하는 것이에요. 종수씨는 취미가 뭐예요?
Mikyung	Je chwiminun chaek iknun kokkwa piano yonsuphanun kos ieyo. Jongsu ssinun chwimiga mwo yeyo?
종수	저는 운동을 좋아해요!
Jongsu	Jonun undongul joahaeyo!
미경	무슨 운동을 좋아해요?
Mikyung	Musun undongul joahaeyo?
종수	저는 축구와 농구를 제일 좋아해요! 등산하는 것도 즐겨요! 미경씨도 운동 좋아해요?
Jongsu	Jonun chukka wa nonggurul jaeil joahaeyo! Tungsanhanun kotto julgyoyo! Mikyung ssido undong joahaeyo?

미경	네! 저도 등산하는 것을 즐겨요. 그리고 테니스도 자주 쳐요. 종수씨는 운동을 왜 좋아해요?
Mikyung	Ne! jodo tungsanhanun kosul julgyoyo. Kurigo tʰenisudo jaju chyoyo. Jongsu ssinun undongul wae joahaeyo?
종수	재미있고 스트레스가 풀려요! 가끔 조금 힘들지만 좋아해요! 그럼 미경씨는 책 읽는 것을 왜 좋아해요?
Jongsu	Jaemi ikko sutʰuresuga pʰullyoyo! Kakkum jogum himduljiman joahaeyo! Kurom Mikyung ssinun chaek iknun kosul wae joahaeyo?
미경	재밌어요! 저는 책 읽는 것이 제일 재밌어요.
Mikyung	Jaemissoyo! Jonun chaek iknun kosi jaeil jaemissoyo.

08.04 Conversation 2

종수	민준씨, 취미가 뭐예요? 운동 좋아해요?
Jongsu	Minjun ssi, chwimiga mwo yeyo? Undong joahaeyo?
민준	제 취미는 운동이에요! 네 운동 정말 좋아해요!
Minjun	Je chwiminun undong ieyo! Ne undong jongmal joahaeyo!
종수	저도 운동 좋아해요! 민준씨는 무슨 운동 좋아해요?
Jongsu	Jodo undong joahaeyo! Minjun ssinun musun undong joahaeyo?
민준	저는 야구를 제일 좋아해요. 탁구도 자주 쳐요. 그리고 한 달에 한 번 등산을 해요! 종수씨는 무슨 운동을 좋아해요?
Minjun	Jonun yagurul jeil joahaeyo. Tʰakkudo jaju chyoyo. Kurigo han dare han bon dungsanul haeyo! Jongsu ssinun musun undongul joahaeyo?
종수	저는 배드민턴을 제일 좋아해요! 낚시와 골프도 즐겨요.
Jongsu	Jonun bedumintʰonul jeil joahaeyo! Nakssiwa golpʰudo julgyoyo.
민준	배드민턴은 얼마나 자주 쳐요?
Minjun	Bedumintʰonun olmana jaju chyoyo?
종수	요즘 배드민턴은 매일 쳐요! 하지만 보통 이틀에 한 번 쳐요.
Jongsu	Yojum bedumintʰonun maeil chyoyo! Hajiman potʰong itʰure han bon chyoyo.
민준	낚시는 얼마나 자주 해요?
Minjun	Nakssinun olmana jaju haeyo?

종수	한 달에 다섯 번 쯤 해요! 낚시가 정말 재밌어요. 낚시하면 기분이 좋아져요. 민준씨는 야구 자주 해요?
Jongsu	Han dare tasot pon jjum haeyo! Nakssiga jongmal jaemissoyo. Nakssihamyon kibuni joajyoyo. Minjun ssinun yagu jaju haeyo?
민준	네 매주 목요일과 토요일에 야구 해요. 건강에 정말 좋아요.
Minjun	Ne maeju mogyoil kwa tʰoyoire yagu haeyo. Kongange jongmal joayo.

UNIT 9

09.02 Conversation 1

민수	철민씨 어제 뭐 했어요?
Minsu	Cholminssi oje mwo haessoyo?
철민	어제 운동했어요.
Cholmin	Oje undong haessoyo.
민수	누구랑 운동했어요?
Minsu	Nugurang undong haessoyo?
철민	중기와 함께 오후에 등산했어요. 재미있었어요! 민수씨는 어제 뭐 했어요?
Cholmin	Junggi wa hamkke ohue tungsan haessoyo. Jaemi issossoyo! Minsu ssinun oje mwo haessoyo?
민수	저는 오전에 집에 있었어요. 청소했어요. 그리고 빨래했어요. 정말 힘들었어요.
Minsu	Jonun ojone jibe issossoyo. Chongso haessoyo. Kurigo ppallae haessoyo. Jongmal himdurossoyo.
철민	오후에는 뭐 했어요?
Cholmin	Ohuenun mwo haessoyo?
민수	동생이랑 점심 먹었어요. 그 다음에 음악 들었어요. 오후에는 한가했어요.
Minsu	Tongsaeng irang jomsim mogossoyo. Ku daume umak turossoyo. Ohuenun hanga haessoyo.

09.04 Conversation 2

민수	오늘 아침에 뭐 했어요? 언제 일어났어요?
Minsu	Onul achime mwo haessoyo? Onje ironassoyo?
철민	아침 일곱시에 일어났어요. 그리고 학교 갔어요. 학교에서 공부했어요. 책도 읽었어요. 민수씨는 언제 일어났어요?

Cholmin	Achim ilgopsie ironassoyo. Kurigo hakkyo kassoyo. Hakkyoeso kongbu haessoyo. Chaekto ilgossoyo. Minsu ssinun onje ironassoyo?
민수	저는 아홉시에 일어났어요. 그리고 오전에 친구 만났어요.
Minsu	Jonun ahop sie ironassoyo. Kurigo ojone chingu mannassoyo.
철민	어디서 만났어요?
Cholmin	Odiso mannassoyo?
민수	안나를 백화점에서 만났어요. 안나와 함께 점심을 먹었어요.
Minsu	Annarul paekʰwajom eso mannassoyo. Anna wa hamkke jomsimul mogossoyo.
철민	오후에는 뭐 했어요?
Cholmin	Ohuenun mwo haessoyo?
민수	오후에는 한가했어요. 집에 있었어요. 집에서 그림 그렸어요. 철민씨는 오후에도 학교 갔어요?
Minsu	Ohuenun hanga haessoyo. Jibe issossoyo. Jibeso kurim kuryossoyo. Cholmin ssinun ohuedo hakkyo kassoyo?
철민	아니요. 오후에는 골프 쳤어요.
Cholmin	Aniyo. Ohuenun kolpʰu chossoyo.
민수	누구랑 쳤어요?
Minsu	Nugurang chossoyo?
철민	형이랑 골프 쳤어요.
Cholmin	Hyong irang kolpʰo chossoyo.

UNIT 10

10.02 Conversation 1

해리	용수씨 주말에 뭐 할 거예요?
Haeri	Yongsu ssi jumare mwo halkkoeyo?
용수	토요일에 약속 있어요. 친구 만날 거예요.
Yongsu	Tʰoyoire yaksok issoyo. Chingu mannal kkoeyo.
해리	어디서 만날 거예요?
Haeri	Odiso mannal kkoeyo?
용수	강남 역 삼 번 출구 앞에서 만날 거예요.
Yongsu	Kangnam yok sam pon chulgu apʰeso mannal kkoeyo.
해리	일요일에는 뭐 할 거예요?
Haeri	Iryoirenun mwo hal kkoeyo?
용수	일요일에는 약속 없어요. 한가해요.

Yongsu	Iryoirenun yaksok opssoyo. Hangahaeyo.
해리	그럼 일요일에 만날까요?
Haeri	Kurom iryoire mannalkkayo?
용수	네! 좋아요! 일요일에 만나요!
Yongsu	Ne! Joayo! Iryoire mannayo!
해리	두시에 백화점 앞에서 만나요! 그때 봐요!
Haeri	Tu sie paekʰwajom apʰeso mannayo! Ku ttae pwayo!

10.04 Conversation 2

지수	다음주 언제 만날까요?
Jisu	Taumju onje mannalkkayo?
다나	목요일에는 일 있어요. 학교 갈 거예요. 수요일에 만날까요?
Dana	Mogyoirenun il issoyo. Hakkyo kalkkoeyo. Suyoire mannalkkayo?
지수	좋아요. 시간 있어요. 수요일에 만나요! 신촌 역에서 만날까요?
Jisu	Joayo. Sigan issoyo. Suyoire mannayo! Sinchon yogeso mannalkkayo?
다나	아니요 버스 정류장에서 만나요! 수요일에 뭐 할까요?
Dana	Aniyo. Posu jongnyujang eso mannayo! Suyoire mwo halkkayo?
지수	저는 축구를 좋아해요. 축구 경기 보러 가요! 어때요?
Jisu	Jonun chukku rul joahaeyo. Chukku kyonggi poro kayo! Ottaeyo?
다나	안 돼요. 저는 축구 싫어해요. 영화 좋아해요?
Dana	Andweyo. Jonun chukku sirohaeyo. Yonghwa joahaeyo?
지수	네 영화 보는 것 좋아해요. 영화 볼까요?
Jisu	Ne yonghwa ponun kot joahaeyo. Yonghwa polkkayo?
다나	네 영화 봐요! 그리고 저녁에는 커피숍 가요!
Dana	Ne yonghwa pwayo. Kurigo jonyogenun kʰopʰi shop kayo!
지수	좋아요! 언제 만날까요?
Jisu	Joayo! Onje mannalkkayo?
다나	네시 반에 만나요. 버스 정류장에서!
Dana	Nesi pane mannayo. Posu jongnyujang eso!
지수	그때 봐요! 안녕히 가세요!
Jisu	Ku ttae pwayo! Annyonghi kaseyo!

Credits

PICTURE CREDITS:

U1 – kurhan/Shutterstock.com

U2 – wizdata/Shutterstock.com

U3 – Maxim Tupikov/Shutterstock.com

U4 – Seet/Shutterstock.com

U5 – wizdata/Shutterstock.com

U6 – Bikeworldtravel/Shutterstock.com

U7 – Bikeworldtravel/Shutterstock.com

U8 – Maxim Tupikov/Shutterstock.com

U9 – 41/Shutterstock.com

U10 – MPFphotography/Shutterstock.com

VOICE CREDITS:

Recorded at Alchemy Studios, London

Cast: Byun-Gon Lee, Hyunsoo Han, Jaehee Cho, Katherine Pageon